Sculpting the Mist

Reports from Elderhood
2019-2021

June O. Underwood

To Shelly
Who is a vital part
of all this

June

For Jer and the real Jan

CONTENTS

PROLOGUE

So——

What is it like to be nearly 80 years old—middlin' old—a developmental stage that comes after "young senior" and before "frail elder."

Strange terms for a new time of life—new, at least, to me.

Mid-elderhood takes place after the bustling years of new retirement and before the aging body is confined to quarters. It's a good chunk of time—years—that we 21st century humans have to enjoy life. It's a subcategory of the more general "elderhood," which is the last of the three stages of human development: childhood, adulthood, and then, elderhood.

Middling-old, this middle stage of elderhood, is an in-between age. It comes when retirement has lost some of its luster: the bucket list has been worked over; one's home has fewer stairs and throw rugs; the trip to the Grand Canyon has come and gone. The grandchildren have grown beyond cuddly, and the great-grands are exhausting. Airports are confusing, driving dangerous, restaurant seats are hard on the backside. Home is quieter and the food is better. And life, with all its meanings, continues.

I am writing here from that middle-old stage. In this writing I am the subject (aged 77, 78, and 79), the researcher (analyzing at age 80 what those last years were like) and the reporter (reviewing and commenting on the material from a later date.)

Sometimes, the life of elders is imagined as consisting mostly of memories. But remembering and living are two very different things. We remember the peaks and abysses of our lives—the romances, the divorces, the birth of children, and the fight with the boss. But experiencing is how we live, regardless of our stage of development. Even as mid-life adults wait for and make memories of peak moments, and children anticipate Christmas and build sentiments around sunlit summers, most of life is lived with morning coffee and the first dandelion. For middle-elders, the goals and strivings have generally passed; peaks and abysses have smoothed out. And, waiting is tedious because it isn't waiting in anticipation of something better. The best of life, for us, resides in the joys of the day.

Those bits of dailiness are what I wrote about, starting in 2019. Few memory-making moments jumped out at me during the couple of years that I jotted daily reports. But what I learned was (forgive the word) profound.

Writing confirmed that I had to live in the moment. I had to experience each day as it came: there was nothing to wait for; Christmas wasn't going to be more magical than July 23; I was not going to make it to CEO or win the Nobel Prize. If pleasure and meaning were to appear, it would be in the everyday. If I were to understand what it was all about, I had to make my own shapes of meaning. To do that I had to experience rather than remember.

During those few years, as I sat down to write, I asked myself: "What can I say about the last 24 hours?"

And then I would recount one thing, or ten, recording something of those lived hours, making stories, anecdotes, speaking of friends and neighbors, and flowers.

The original notes were written from June 2019 to March 2021. It was a relatively stable world when I began. Then came the world pandemic, the American Insurrection, and personal surgical events. Life, as it is *wont to do, moved along. But this daily record is how bits of my life were actually experienced, during those years of middlin' elderhood.*

Then, a couple of years later, I reflected on what I had written.

The later notes are in italics after various entries. They were written to clarify questions about language and situations within the entries, but they also respond to that most querulous earworm: "So what?"

"So what" has not yet been thoroughly resolved. There's still time. At this writing, I'm only 80, still middlin' old, not yet frail, so there's time.

A note about format: the writing, with its dates, may seem like journal entries. However, they are addressed to someone—"Dear Jan."

The "Dear Jan" in these entries was an essential, if peculiar, head-game of my own. "Dear Jan" reminded me that that I was chatting someone up, someone who popped in to ask "How was your day?"

I did not want to write about my previous life experiences, nor about the traumas that I, like any middling-old person, have had. I wanted not to do a deep dive into my inner emotional states. I wanted to record what happened on a daily basis in order to understand more fully what life as a kinda-old person was like.

I chose someone I knew well as my imagined listener: the real person is my daughter, Jan. The imagined one is the Listener-Jan. "Dear Jan" shares a lot with the real Jan, but "Dear Jan" is an alter ego, a figment of my imagination. The real Jan had no access to the writing, so what appears to be letters to her are written without her come-backs. The manuscript was never meant to be a memoir or keepsake for future generations. It was a record of my mid-elderhood days, and my more recent thoughts about those days.

"Dear Jan" has a lot in common with Jan Underwood, novelist, retired Spanish instructor, political activist, and beloved daughter, but "Dear Jan" is also a voice in my head, sympathetic and skeptical, funny and

knowledgeable. Of course, Jan Underwood is also sympathetic and skeptical, funny and knowledgeable, but I'm sure her responses to what I say here would be wittier and more delicious than anything I imagined. If it helps, you can think these notes were letters to you: Dear Ralph, Dear Maggie, Dear Eliza, Dear Beloved.

Along the way, another beloved has helped me with these writings: he is my 81-year-old editor, Jerry Underwood, who is also sympathetic, skeptical, funny, and knowledgeable, as well as being a good cook, and the love of my life.

I
KINWORK, NEIGHBORING, AND THE QUOTIDIAN

The quotidian is not a cotillion. Thank heavens! —John Saling

June 3, 2019
On the Fridge

Dear Jan,

On our refrigerator, scrawled on small pieces of paper and attached with the usual hodge-podge of magnets, are names—people names, dog names, cat names, names with question marks.

These bits and pieces began in 2014 and they continue through last week. When we moved to the Montavilla neighborhood in 2014, we were determined to learn the new streets and those who lived along them. We walked down the busy avenues and up the unpaved gravel lanes. We nodded, smiled and chatted with everyone we passed. People asked our names; we asked theirs. And when we got home, we wrote down names and stuck them on the fridge. The resulting accumulations have become post-it notes of our current universe.

Each name represents a moment when Jer and I greeted someone and, perhaps, after pleasantries about weather, street cleanings, onion snows, and can-gatherers, would progress to introductions. We would exchange first names, maybe gesture toward where we lived ("just up the street," "around the corner," "over on 86th"), be introduced to the lurking or lounging dog or cat, and as we moved on down the street, we would remind each other of the names we just learned: Mike and Merlo and—what was *her* name—ah—Kristin. Martha—oh, she looks like a most pleasant Martha! Jake is the yellow cat; Binx is the sly one. Angie is outgoing; Donna the introvert. Gepetto lives with Mike and Linda. Gavin and family with Augie? Arlene and John: John an ex-husband—new husband is Richard.

Some of these people we still see and talk with; some have disappeared. One set of children who jumped on the trampoline outside the grandparents' house, we called Five, Six, and Seven. Those were their ages and what they bragged of, yelled at us as we passed, even before they told us their names. We passed them often, admiring their bouncing, rolling, and somersaulting gymnastics. We teased by calling them by their ages, and they teased back by shouting out their names; those names too are on the fridge, although Five, Six, and Seven are what we know them as. After a couple of years, though, they grew too old for the trampoline: it still sits, untended, in the front lawn.

Julie, the dog walker, has a revolving group of dogs, including the bulldog Cash, whose snuffle we hear as he heaves into view. Our favorite Julie dog is the basset hound, Elvis, who greets everyone with loud bays. Julie talks to the dogs constantly, but is shy around people; we talk to her dogs and smile at her, and while she looks mostly at the sidewalk, she acknowledges our good will with a sideways smile.

Others on those bits of paper are now close friends, people who have us to dinner and who join us for drinks on the patio during summer evenings. We have not edited the fridge notes since we moved here, and so regardless of how well we know these people—John and Susan, Mary and Dan, Kerri and David—they are still on their note cards.

The numbers of jottings expand—Lynne Joy and Roger were the last humans added, but a dog or two has since come onto the list. The slips of paper represent messy, catch-as-catch-can life, all around us. Incomplete, for sure, and sometimes mysterious (whoever is Greg Burrel?) but more often, part of our lives, our quotidian, as much a part of our lives as are the fir trees and little square houses that we stroll past.

Love,
Momma

Making sense of a new place felt essential to us when we moved at age 72. This new place is where we might spend our remaining years. We wanted to root ourselves in the space and place, and to do so required intentionality. We needed to know the cats and dogs and chickens, the children and their parents, the adults, the ageing, and the aged. We needed nodding acquaintances, dining friends, storytellers and knowledge of where birds assembled. Even the upheaved sidewalks and puddle-laden back lanes became part of our knowledge of street trees and city ordinances.

Montavilla, our new space, is a 1950s 'burb, built on hilly farmland, just beyond where the 1920s Portland streetcar line stopped. A few older farmhouses still sprinkle the neighborhood, but most of the houses started out as four-room boxes, modest ranch houses. Seventy years later, of course, they have added upper stories, bumped out rooms, and put on porches. The knoll that sits at the center of Montavilla contains a ridge where the wind whips hard in the winter. It has odd streets that curve around the hill with houses that sometimes are odd shaped in themselves. It's American vernacular, contractor-built, mostly working-class housing, upgraded (or sometimes degraded) and fascinating to newbies who walk around imagining what the original spaces must have looked like in 1949.

The only way we could make sense of our new place was to walk it, making doglegs through streets, speaking to everyone and everything we encountered, from toddlers to crows. And of course, we did this not just to grow roots; we found it a good way to enjoy the moments we were living in.

June 10, 2019
Discordant Mixes

Dear Jan,

Beginning with that repetition, Dear Jan, feels like a new beginning, and I love beginnings. Writing down the daily events allows stories to emerge, stories that I'm always trying to understand more fully.

So, Dear Jan, I thought I'd note that yesterday the new drip hose was repositioned and did a fine job of watering the concrete sidewalk as well as the front flower bed.

And before watering the front garden and sidewalk, Jer and I went to Monti's Café, down through the neighborhood to Stark Street, a busy boulevard, where, as old customers at Monti's we generally find cheer, comfort and good coffee.

When we walked in, Elise greeted us with a big smile and handed me an envelope. "June and Jerry," it said, in sprawling handwriting. Opening it, we found a Monti's certificate for $50. It was signed "Anouk"—a thank-you for taking care of Anouk the cat while Susan and John Saling, friends and neighbors, were out of town. The gift would buy at least three meals at Monti's.

We had come to Monti's to shoo away a bit of a funk. Jer was arranging some medical tests, and the systems set up to arrange them seemed opaque, arcane, ridiculous. Setting up medical tests is annoying at best; they remind one of illness and potential pain. To have obstacles in the way of the process—well, we had hoped some strong coffee and cheerful staff chatter would relieve us of our own thoughts. The gift from Susan was a good omen.

But then, we found the staff was having a difficult day. Someone dropped a tray of glasses and swore—loudly. Jessica brought out the wrong salad for people sitting near us and was chided in a fake sweet voice. The French roast coffee ran out, and a loud male voice informed the female staff that he wanted some. Now!

So, sitting with our tuna sandwiches and coffee, nibbling on the thick chewy chips that hurt my gums, we found ourselves loved and a bit out of sorts. Whap, whap, whap went my emotions. First *this* was good, then *that* was not. Back and forth, like pickles and cherries. No stability of mood at all.

But then Jer and I talked about the appointment difficulties and sorted out some strategies for navigating the systems. Our French roast coffee, fresh-made with good cream, took hold. Our moods lifted; the café emptied out, and the staff chattered and laughed within a quiet respite. We walked home in the sunshine.

In other words, it was a day in which moods were all over the place, bing, bang, bong. This morning, I note that the repositioned hose had watered the front sidewalk as well as the front flowerbed. I re-repositioned it.

Each of these little missives gives me ways to walk through time. Writing provides me a tool to explain, at least to myself, how my thoughts are binging and banging and rummaging and ruminating—and sometimes, merely repositioning themselves.

Mama

June 15, 2019
Dust-up at the Farmers Market

Dear Jan,

Life is full of incidents that tickle my fancy.

We were at the Saturday farmers market yesterday, picking through the baskets of strawberries and eyeing the early blueberries. In front of me was a 30-something woman waiting in line to pay; off to one side was a dog, a stroller, two children, another woman, and a storm of sound and fury. The two-year-old (male), sitting in the stroller, was kicking his three-year-old sibling (female) who was perched in front of him. He was big for his age, and she was rather small. He was restless, wanting to be out, wanting attention. She was watching a puppy sniffing at her mama's feet. So, the action began: first the younger sibling launched a flurry of little kicks at his sister, and then, when she failed to respond, he issued one big blow, delivered with both feet. The little girl fell over on her face.

Oh my, such a hullaballoo. Mama, abandoning her boxes of berries, ran to see what the howling was about. The other adult confronted the offender, sternly. The injured one with the (invisible) owie was held and calmed by the first mama. The little male was unfazed by the chiding, the female child disappointed by the lack of blood. Both children were abruptly distracted when handed strawberries. They mashed the berries into their mouths, looking around as if to wonder what all the fuss was about.

Most satisfying. Brothers and sisters, engaging one another for ends that are slightly mysterious but clearly important—these have been around forever. And those strawberries, mashed through teeth amidst snot and tears—those too feel eternal.

I am easily amused. My fancy was tickled.

Love,
Mama

The phrase "tickle my fancy" is old-fashioned as well as a bit of a cliché. However, it may now ring fresh because scarcely anyone gets their fancy tickled any more. That's the way with clichés—they sometimes bob up a hundred years later and look all cleaned up.

You may have noticed that on June 3 I used the phrase "onion snow." "Onion snow" is an old-fashioned term for a late spring snow, very wet, which falls after the onion sets have been planted. The onion snow is said to harden and water the new onion sets. I like it because it defines and thus gives a bit of meaning to those late snows which occur so regularly in Portland, Oregon. I also find it a good way to discuss the weather with people we meet on our walks; they move from the clichés of "wintry mixes, ugh," to "What's an inion snow?"

June 23, 2019
Matters of Daily Delights

Dear Jan,

It becomes necessary, just because, to record some of the fine moments of my day.

First, during our daily step-count walk, a young guy drove by, rap blaring, tattooed arm hanging out of his beat-up Toyota window. He glanced at me, smiled, and waved as I picked my way along 86th Avenue. Around the corner and down the unpaved street, an old gent (10 years younger than us) grinned and then rearranged his features to look ironic as we admired his gardening. Binx, the unsociable cat, glared when I spoke to him, but his sibling, Jake, rubbed against my leg and whispered his hellos. We walked on, turning the corner to find the usual street urchin basketball game in progress. The kids stopped fighting over the ball and waved hellos as I wandered through their asphalt court. The kids aren't really urchins, but gregarious, working-class 10-year-olds, who always greet us when we walk by. I admired their jump shots and remembered a couple names.

And then, into the car for an outing: we drove up the river to Rose Villa, the retirement community where Cousin Marilyn lives. She is new to Portland and her community and, at age 74, thinking about the nature of aging and its many transitions. Marilyn is one of the youngest and handsomest creatures in her continuing care community, but, to state the obvious, she *is* aging. So we discussed theories of "how we live" and "what we do now" and "which parts will go first." We had ham sandwiches at the community's restaurant, looking out over a blossoming patio into sprinkles of rain.

Finally, after returning from Marilyn's, I rescued an unidentified plant from under the eaves. It was dry and droopy, but its wilting blooms sat up and looked around as I dribbled water over them. Maybe it will live another day or two.

And so, the daily delights of attending one's garden and one's kin, of flirting with a passing motorist, and of checking out cats and short basketball players -- these are the mundane, yet crucial shapes of aging.

Yer Ma,
Mama

July 4, 2019
The Stuff of Life

Dear Jan,

Every year on July 4, I am reminded of an old saying: "Bread is the staff of life." Breaking bread together, eating with friends and family, is the stuff both of memory and experience.

Five years and a day ago, we moved from 14th and Main to 86th Avenue, from the big four-square century-old house close to the river to this story-and-a-half box that resembles the other Levittown-look-alike houses in this 70-year-old suburban neighborhood.

It was the spaciousness of the Main Street house that pushed us out. Our arthritic knees complained about climbing steps to the bedrooms and the basement; I worried about the dust collecting in the unused guest room, and the big wooden table was too large for the two of us.

So we decided to leave the big magnolia, the shore pine, the spare bedroom where out-of-town friends could spend the night, the claw-footed table that filled the family room, the front parlor and formal dining room where I did textile art—we left it for this little square house in the middle of the block, a surprise of a house, with a bright bump-out room for books and music and the nook with a dining room table that can seat 10 people if we squeeze a little.

I remember well the day we moved here, the 3rd of July, 2014. We were worn out with months of packing and paper-work, exasperated with one other, and fussed about all the delays. The new owners for the Main Street house were eager to move over the 4th of July weekend. The guy who sold us the 86th Avenue place had only just finished packing his last boxes and mopping the kitchen floor on July 2nd. It was hot. Tempers were frayed.

At 7:30 on the morning of July 3rd, you and Rick took my art materials and inventory to the new garage studio, emptied late the night before by the previous owner. We had the com-puters and a suitcase of clothes in the car, as well as coffee making materials and a bottle of wine. We were ready to go.

But our movers, a couple of guys with a big truck and a good reputation, called at 10 to say they wouldn't be coming at 8 AM, but rather, they would arrive by noon. At 3 PM, they called again to say they were running late.

We were frantic, thinking we had chosen the wrong movers, that disaster loomed, that it was a catastrophe. But, at 5 PM, here they were! Out the door went mattresses and head-boards, couch and tables and chairs. Pots and pans, boxes of books, heavy things we couldn't move, and light things we couldn't live without—all packed into the big truck by two young guys. It was evening and then night and the trudging and carrying went on.

By 11 PM, however, the loaded truck trundled off to 86th Avenue; we followed, and the two guys unpacked and carried everything into the new house. Boxes were piled—mostly in the designated rooms—and the beds were made-up with sheets and blankets. We were close to being done, although, even in our exhausted state, we felt like monsters, knowing the two twenty-some-year-old kids had worked through a 16-hour day. They hadn't stopped for dinner, although they assured us that they were "fine."

Then came the knock on the door.

It was Susan, from across the street, the friend who had found us the house. There she was, bags dangling and paper plates in hand.

She had brought cookies, drinks, sandwiches, and more—enough for an army of movers and pitiful homeowners—enough for three nights of dining while we searched for the spatula to cook eggs.

It was food, it was life-saving, and we ate together—the moving guys, Susan, all of us, sitting on the floor among packing boxes. It felt like this was a place we could stay forever.

On Main Street we had a stately beautiful residence; on 86th Avenue in Montavilla, we have neighbors and friends and a beflowered and sunshiny house. We feed people readily, and we have friends who know when we need fed.

Love,
Mama

When we were a young married couple with one child, we moved easily and often. At one point, when I was about 35, I counted 19 different places we had lived in since we got married 13 years before; apartments and houses in Pennsylvania, Virginia, Wyoming, New York, and Kansas.

One result of moving so often is that I am acutely aware of the space and place and people where I live. As young newlyweds, we moved out *of one house in State College, Pennsylvania because the septic tank leaked, making a sewage pond behind the house. Another ramshackle rental on Cherry Lane in State College was across the lawn from our landlord's house; he was a construction worker and decorated both places with cast-off paint from his work. He lowered our rent from $75 a month to $60 when Jan was born. In Laramie, Wyoming, where we had lived in at least five different houses, our last home was on Rainbow Avenue; we paneled the basement with bark from beetle-damaged trees. I could describe every space in the rambling 100-year-old Kansas house we all loved; I can still see the fading wallpaper behind the stove where we accidentally roasted a mouse. The house on Main Street here in Portland is catty-cornered from a former brothel and next to a low-income boarding house. Now, east of 82nd Avenue, we live in a one-story nest, next door to a toddler and his kin, and on the other side, a couple of young boys with friendly parents. I have lived and loved in all kinds of spaces; each one had its own charms and its own challenges. Now we are settled into a snug, well-maintained house where the neighbors feed us and we are welcomed.*

July 7, 2019
Adventures: Definitions and Expositions

Dear Jan,

It's the kind of day when I stand in the doorway and watch the world go by. The static world (flowers, sidewalk, grass strip, ash tree, parking space, street) can suddenly flair with movement and energy.

Today it was a mama with a stroller, flanked by a young dog, and a just-past-two-year-old, moseying erratically down the street. Suddenly the dog ran toward the street and the toddler waddled toward the yard to snatch a flower's head. The leash tangled with the stroller and around mama's feet—mama bent and turned first toward the dog, then grabbed at the thieving child who wobbled, unbalanced by the pansy he was holding. Mama looked bewildered and bemused. The dog detected an enticing odor in the parking strip and stopped to investigate. The child found a pine cone to eat. It reminded me of times when you saw a world full of excitement—tasting a pine cone, squeezing a dead sock, throwing a smooth round rock at a yellow flower—and I juggled a stroller, diaper bag, and an escaping toddler. Those hanging-on-days were times that I *knew* adventure was where I wasn't—the Italian alps and German castles maybe, or exploring the ruins of Athens and studying under a brilliant, elegant scholar—adventure happened there, not where I chased the kid and changed the cat box.

Wondering if licking a pine cone would give the kid diarrhea was a worry, not an adventure. But now, years later, I can see that having you bouncing around my legs while we explored the Virginia neighborhood where we lived was definitely adventurous—for you, if not for me.

Earlier this summer we were talking about you and your husband Rick's travel plans.

You and Rick, you said, are going in August to backpack across Isle Royale in Lake Superior, a five-day trip with only what you can carry on your back and lots of blackfly repellant. I responded with descriptions about our latest walks to Monti's, navigating busy Burnside Street, mewling cats, and the new server at the café.

"Daily adventures," I said, trying for a transition from your extended hike in the Midwest.

You said, cheerfully, that backpacking for five days among the bug-ridden Michigan wilds was an *adventure. My* notion of adventure was not quite up to the definition. Jer rather agreed with you and even I had (silent) doubts. However, the conversation moved on to the nature of yellow cats vs. black and white ones, and I had to stop thinking about definitions in order to defend yellow tabbies.

But today, I'm thinking about adventures and how our ideas about them might change as we age. I am definitely having an adventure in writing these notes. I never wrote in this format, speaking to someone whose voice I can hear, answering me back, challenging me and extending my ideas. Each day is singular in its writing challenges: deciding what I can shape from yesterday's ramble often makes me stumble. I go down wrong paths and have to backtrack. I delete whole pages of crappy material and wonder why I ever thought I could do this.

But I still find adventure in our dailiness. During the walks that Jer and I take, questions loom: will Batman, the mongrel dog down the street, jump the fence and sink his teeth into my ankle? Will Binx, the black cat, stop glaring at us and come out to say hello? At home we are learning to cook differently because the Blue Apron food kits come with odd spices and odder words and instructions. I now know what *"fond"* is and why *"mise en place"* is an essential concept. We are never certain that the meal will be edible (operator error is a big factor), and occasionally we smash bowls on the floor in our haste to grab the smoking pan.

The gardens provide a constant flux of challenge and anxiety—are we watering correctly? Is the astilbe getting too much sun? Is there a bare spot of earth that needs enlarged for this new hydrangea? Even more of a challenge, is our kinwork—with you and Grandson Sam and Rick, and the neighbors whom we know well or merely in passing—everyone needing lots of attention, soothing and clucking, and checking out. Shall we drop off a bouquet for Janet? Does Mel seem to be in a funk? What good story can we tell to enliven our dinner with the Adams? What kinds of questions will draw out shy Mr. Lebatte?

These are our adventures at age seventy-eight. It's their freshness, their unexpectedness, their ways to go wrong, that makes them so. So, perhaps "adventure" is something that can only be defined by the individual who experiences the newness, the terror, the exhilaration.

Of course, in former years, I had conventional adventures. Ten years ago, when I was 67, I spent the cold months of February and November painting in the Mojave Desert, working alone at the Red Barn, four miles outside of Beatty, Nevada. Those six-week endeavors were vastly different from *plein air* painting in Portland. The Red Barn, huge and unheated, was half a mile from the road, had tarantulas, a resident desert rat, scary local characters who checked me out in mostly friendly ways, and the desert itself. The desert, greasewood, cacti, unexpected swales, and vicious scrub bushes, as well as the unceasing blue sky and sun, never left me alone—not for a moment. It was scary. It was new and exciting.

Here, ten years later, the adventure is that the chaos of the quotidian, the mush of ordinary life, must be pushed and pulled into some kind of shape. That's hard, demanding work, full of ways to go wrong.

Dictionary.com defines "adventure" as an exciting or unusual experience. In elderhood, adventure can still exist, even if it doesn't (generally speaking) involve sailing the deep blue seas, backpacking for seventy miles across a desolate island, or sniffing trees for evidence of other dogs. Excitement can be had right in one's living room, argufying with one's daughter. You challenge me, and I respond, and off we go, with Jer giving an opinion or two, and the sunlight coming through the window. From your seat, you see who is walking by, and you watch a dog sniff the peony, and the kid pick up a pebble and throw it at the stroller, and a mom laugh and grab the child and swing her around.

Adventures, to my current mind, exist in the hearts and minds of those involved; life at 77 hasn't narrowed to a rocking chair boredom, no matter how it might seem to outsiders.

Yer contrarian Mom

Living with a family that loves language makes talking as adventurous as any trek through the wilderness. And being a middling-elder really does mean that I have to think about old words in a new life.

My family casts a cold eye on my notions, which makes the discussions all the more fun. But having language, even old language, to describe events never so described before, adds a touch of spice to my life, makes me sit up and declaim instead of sitting around looking weary. Language is one way of getting to adventures in our elderhood life.

July 10, 2019
Just Do It

Dear Jan,

It's a muggy, warm July day, more suited for Pennsylvania than Oregon. It rained last night, unusual for July. As an elder, I fuss about weather changes—cold seems colder, heat hotter. And muggy—well, muggy is sleepier. And smellier. When humidity hits, all the odors get deep and sticky. Science tells us that as we age, our biological systems find it harder to adjust to outside physical changes. I'm certain the science is correct. But I would add that mental and emotional adjustments are harder, also.

I'm much more of a worrier now than I ever was. In my 40s, 50s, 60s, I blew off a lot of things, particularly the "small" stuff. "Don't sweat the small stuff." "This too will pass." "Don't trouble trouble 'till trouble troubles you." These were the kinds of sayings that I blithely passed along. But now, I sweat a lot of small events; I forget that life is about change and flux; I fuss about the troubles that might happen. I worry about whether *this* morning I will have anything to write about. I worry about whether today I will reach my 7,000-step goal, mandated for elder-health; I worry that the daylilies out front need deadheading.

Of course, the daylilies will need blooms removed. They are in their full glory, which means that yesterday's blooms will be today's desiccated flowers. Flopping flowers must be removed to make room for new ones. In the meantime, August, a very hot, brown month, is coming. The pansies must be depotted and planted in the coolest spot in the gardens, where they may or may not survive. If they go down with heat exhaustion, what we will find to replace them? And what if we don't get the new things planted before the heat gets worse? And what if, because of the vicious temperatures (the imagination always ratchets up), the new things all die?

Did I mention I've become a worrier?

However, here I am. I have already walked 4,000 steps and the bum knee is just fine. The worry has turned into words and the words turned into images. One big oriental lily near the studio door has stretched its petals and widened them away from its sheath. The flowers grow, bud, bloom, and are deadheaded; I put on sweaters and take them off, find a lighter weight blouse, and shed my blue jeans for shorts. Although I've turned into a worrier, I am also keen to adapt to whatever comes along. As elders we adjust—turning to face the sun or kneeling to plant new offerings to the shade.

Love you,
Mom

July 29, 2019

Kinwork, or How to Talk to Chickens.

Dear Jan,

Our immediate circle of kin and kinwork has enlarged. Among those I think of as kin, accepting our presence as their due, are the animals around us.

Jer has long been adept at talking to cats. I have tried to imitate him, but he is the master. The other day, I realized he's learned chicken-speak. On our daily walk to Monti's there are three chickens: LaVerne, Patty, and Maxene. I have long thought that the only language chickens know is the feeding call: a high-pitched "chick, chick, chick." Chickens are too stupid to come in out of the rain (so old wives tell me). And chickens don't like you, they don't want you to take their eggs, and they fly at you and peck at your hands and make a loud ruckus, terrifying the kid sent to get the eggs for supper.

But Jer, who has little or no previous chicken experience, talks to these chickens every day. He doesn't try to imitate them, although he changes his voice tones, depending on what they are doing. And he detects a change in the chickens' bearing when we near their enclosure.

I am aware, as he may not be, that the kitchen window of the chickens' people is right above their pen, and that they (the people) were perhaps first disturbed and now have become bemused at the chicken chat from the bearded old guy. Sometimes they appear and greet us and tell us about the character of an individual fowl—Maxene is always the noisiest one.

We go on the same walk every day so the kinwork is familiar. The yellow cat now accepts both of us equally, although originally it was Jer he responded to. In the spring, a certain pair of crows becomes belligerent, warning us to keep clear of their nests. Jer speaks to all the dogs, even those that charge the fence at us. His "hello woof" calms *me*, even if some of the dogs continue to growl. The scary dogs are confined, and Jer can do his kinwork, both for them and for me.

However, I am the one more likely to talk to the kids and adults along the route. I admire the new shasta daisy at Darlene's house and wave to the four-year-old sitting with grandpa on their front deck. Darlene tells me of the other things she has planted in the brick-hard soil of the space between the sidewalk and the street. The four-year-old tells me about the book grandpa is reading to her. Jer admires the dogs—Chihuahua or pit bull—that accompany the people we pass and in asking their names and speaking dog-talk to them, he wins everyone's hearts. And so, we become friends with a whole community of living things; we do our kinwork.

On these walks, Jer and I talk of personal things too, our arthritic knees, our general gripes about the nation's and our own health, and our hopes—for ourselves and our various kin.

These daily routines create our web of community. They are essential, even when those involved are unaware of their uses. They hold a community together in a light web of common interests and civility, one which can be broken or lost, but can also be rebuilt and held stable. Kinwork of all sorts, is essential to the mental well-being of society. And ourselves.

Mama

August 20, 2019
Kinwork

Dear Jan,

You and Rick are probably on a flight to Portland, coming back from Isle Royale and Lake Superior and a couple of baseball games. We'll be glad to see you safe in PDX; somehow it seems safer when you are here in town, not in some mysterious place halfway across the country.

We were at the Salings' last night for their 49th wedding anniversary, which they traditionally celebrate with a sit-down dinner.

There were ten or twelve of us present—strangers when we first started going to these anniversary affairs, but now friends. Mary Lane, your friend and then mine, sat beside me.

I asked, as one does, what she was up to.

"Nothing," she said.

I raised an eyebrow, and she said no, really, I'm just reading and walking around the neighborhood, admiring the cats, and checking to see who's home and which neighbor needs to cut their grass. We laughed, and I said "Kinwork."

She looked puzzled. So I explained that we Underwoods have pushed the term beyond its anthropological, blood-relative designation, to mean being attentive to everyone we connect with, however briefly—people like the cashiers at Safeway and the servers at Monti's, dog owners, cat people, gardeners, neighborhood denizens whose paths we cross—the secondary and tertiary people who compose so much of our lives. The network of neighborhood community makes a kinship that goes well beyond the immediate kin and kinwork of family and friends.

Mary Lane is the perfect maker of connections. She is curious about everything she comes across. She has firm opinions (good ones for the most part) but isn't offensive with them. She is quick to laugh, at herself most of all. Everyone gravitates toward her, which is why she's so good at kinwork.

She was quite pleased to have a name for what she's been doing in her seemingly desultory summer of wandering around the neighborhood. The naming of the activity gave her pleasure and a sense of usefulness.

The table broke up and people moved about. A batch of the women, and a couple of men gravitated toward the kitchen, so I followed them. I expected to find them cleaning up dishes, but instead, they were discussing books, swapping recommendations, laughing at titles, delighted at their mutual love of language.

I was momentarily startled that the group wasn't washing silverware, but that's because in my old family, the kinwork was done during after-dinner clean-up—washing and drying the dishes, putting leftovers into the refrigerator, discussing the kids and yard sales, who had gone to the doctor, and where they were going camping next week. Here, 60-odd years later, my current "kin" are making literary and intellectual connections that will carry them through their smaller families and smaller duties of the next weeks or months.

Before we left, Mary Lane checked on your status, and I got to tell her you would be home tomorrow. We will get together on Friday, I said, so we can hear Rick's recounting of the major league game and your take on the camping trip and what you both read in your downtime there. Kinship at its most fundamental.

Hugs,
Mama

August 21, 2019
Days and Ways

Dear Jan,

Rituals to begin writing can be useful. My rituals—writing or doing art—involve opening the studio. I turn on the radio to the All Classical station, click on the hot pot to make tea, boot up the computer, and go to email. Then I tidy the snacks from the previous day, rinse my cup, and put bits of notes to myself in the recycling wastebasket.

I can draw out this sequence by checking on the plants outside, noting the weather, deadheading a flower or two—procrastinating, but only up to a point.

Today the rituals also involve dealing with the physical knocks that accompany this stage of development. A friend emails about her aortic valve replacement and I email her a "congratulations;" a letter of condolence, to a friend from 35 years or so ago, needs written. On the phone I walk one of our friends through her list of ailing friends; at the end, she says her own summer has been wonderful, a comment that rounds her news in a positive way. Rituals of friendship, observed by both parties.

And so, one gets up, makes tea, confronts the day, tidies the appliances, and attends to kinwork. The sun comes out, a cat brushes against your skin, and a stranger smiles at you. Some rituals are big, ponderous, done by public institutions like the church, and they signify major transitions. But most of my rituals are mundane, ways to navigate ways and time. I take comfort in them sometimes and sometimes I twitch at their humdrum nature. But the rituals are patient and wait for me.

Mama

August 22, 2019
Ambience

Dear Jan,

After you left from our Friday morning check-in, Jer and I moseyed to Monti's to have our coffee, mingle with the staff, and talk about the ideas and stories you had showered us with.

Monti's is a good place for conversations. The bookcases that line the walls make it easy to talk in—neither too quiet nor too noisy. It's a place where people meet for working sessions on their new project or to conduct job interviews.

Sometimes we hear an older woman explaining to a newbie how she navigates the pitfalls at the office. A pastor is often seen guiding young men along the path that his religion suggests good men and women follow. He's gentle and a listener, and his audience is often young, earnest, and desperate. Middle-aged people come to try to figure out what to do with Mama; she's mentally good but she's fallen five times. Elders like us chat with friends and rummage around the books. The old guy who tends the shelves brings in new books and puts them out, lightly organized. The workers at the attached antique marketplace come in for late lunches. A few mamas bring children, babies, husbands, to munch on big cookies, cookies in white wax bags out of which they can be nibbled. At 9 AM a shift of police supervisors takes over one of the big tables; in the afternoon, there are mimosa drinkers. And there's always a couple of people playing cards; less often, a lone soul will be playing solitaire and sipping a latte.

In short, Monti's is a place for locals, but even more, a place for people who want human contact. The books are a great resource for those who read while they eat. The antique store's music, which we can hear in the café, is played at just the right level, and it's mostly 40s and 50s crooners of jazz and big band vocalists. The servers who mingle with the kitchen staff, who at times *are* the kitchen staff, are friendly but not intrusive—they bring you the food you've ordered and paid for at the counter, and then forget how long you've stayed. The number of free refills on the coffee varies with who's serving, but Jer and I were told early on that at least three cups were acceptable. No one seems to notice how many trips we make.

Face-to-face is Monti's specialty, although I bet they imagine it's their chicken and cranberry sandwich on a croissant that's the draw. The sandwiches are OK, the coffee superb, the mimosas a treat, but really, it's the place and the people that make it our go-to home.

Mama

Oct 10, 2019

A Listing of Plants

Dear Jan,

We planted about 200 tulip bulbs last weekend. The number feels outrageous, because I've put in either too many -- or not enough.

We have a lot of gardens, independent spaces shaped out with plants for year-round interest. The most important season for me is tulip time—mid-March through early May. Every little space in and around already planted areas can hold a tulip or 10, so no matter how many bulbs I get I always think, when they bloom, they are too few.

Out front, three boxes fill the "parking" (that 10-foot strip between the street and the sidewalk)—they get a few daffodils to catch the eye. The large flower bed that was once a front lawn is where the majority of tulips get stuffed. That bed holds other spring flowers, a big Australian bottle bush, a dogwood tree, and a mammoth hydrangea. It also has summer and fall bloomers, so the tulips are snuggled in and around perennials that just peep out of dark soil while the tulips bounce and bloom. The triangular dogwood bed, between porch, driveway and walk to the front, gets crocuses.

In the back the deck containers hold forsythia, pieris, tuberous begonia, and 10 or 15 other miscellaneous plants; I always plant bulbs in pots there because we look out at the space and need our spring color. The hellebore, lobelia, violets, and Korean fern surround the fountain off the deck, sharing space with hyacinths and fritillaria. The big ceramic pots in front of the studio and the fulsome daylily bed across the side of the studio leave no room for bulbs, but I can always find a way to tuck some into the lily/salvia/lilac bed in front of the library window, as well as into the bed under the persimmon tree, the narrow border along the back driveway, and Jer's west-side parking and upper beds.

So many spaces. So few tulips and daffs and hyacinth and fritallia to fill them. I see I need to order more.

Mama

So why did I list these nooks and crannies into which I snuggle plants and bulbs? First, it's a pleasure just to enumerate them. This list enumerates shapes that we have worked on, dug out, sculpted from formless grounds; we made these shapes so they can contain life. And the list highlights beauty to watch for as the seasons come round. Spring will follow winter; crocuses and blueberries will bloom and fruit. Life will continue, regardless of human chaos.

December 24, 2019
Monti's Café Culture

Dear Jan,

We walked slowly down to Monti's today, Christmas Eve Day, and as usual I eavesdropped on the customers.

Monti's, the day before Christmas, has a different vibe. There are no tykes or babies to wink at; no job seekers laying out their computer skills for the director of the badly-funded non-profit; no spiritual seekers, gazing into the eyes of the Reverend. And not many other oldsters on their weekly outing.

No, the two tables of diners that I observed (not counting the young man reading the book about cactus while stroking his well-shaved head) were those with bags of packages, some wrapped, some not. The crinkling of wrapping paper and gentle squeals of thank-yous accompanied presents, exchanged among friends who had met here just for that purpose.

In the past we have observed many people being given presents in Monti's. Once it was a ring exchange between a couple of gray-hairs just a few years younger than us. Sometimes it's birthdays, young and old, where the recipient isn't part of the family, and so the gift is given in a public place. Sometimes it's a huge cookie with a candle stuck in its icing, accompanied by jokes and laughter.

This is a place where people seem to say, "thanks for being part of my life."

I'm thinking perhaps we should host Jer at Monti's for his 80th birthday, buy him a tuna fish sandwich and a smoothie. Not a cluttered gathering nor evening affair. No best shirt and clean jeans required. Just Monti's, surrounded by used and sometimes musty books, good coffee smells, people who may or may not live in the neighborhood but who know this is a place where good relationships form and are kept.

So Merry, Merry Christmas Eve to you, my love, and just in case you don't know—comfort for me also exists in knowing where you are in your life-filled, ever-fascinating rooms, where cats wander and leap on laps. Our comfort is in Monti's and in our own living room with the gas fire on a cold winter's night. Good spaces all 'round.

Mama

January 13, 2020
Old-Person's Projects and the New Coffee Machine

Dear Jan,

John McPhee identifies why he—and I—continue to pursue projects that aren't quite rational. As long as we are working on projects, we aren't dead yet.

My motive for writing these reports is that I prefer old to dead.

But what has that to do with a new coffeepot?

I refer you to Roz Chast's graphic novel: *Can't we talk about something more PLEASANT?*

Chast recounts the last 10 or so years of her parents' lives; she, as the only child, is charged with helping them as they age. Chast's parents believed (as do we) in keeping things as long as they still have some useful life left: Her example is an oven mitt "from the year one" with patches from "a skirt I made forty years ago in Home Ec!"

"Please let me buy you a new oven mitt."

"Why waste your money? That one still works."

It was after reading Roz Chast that I decided we needed a new coffeepot.

Our last automatic coffee maker was a Mr. Coffee, bought in 1964. In Pennsylvania, in 1964, coffee was only slightly darker than tea, and made in the Mr. Coffee. It invariably dripped on the warming plate, filling the kitchen with burnt bean smell. In my mother's house, the coffeepot sat on the warming plate all day, where it turned from lightly-flavored slosh to burn-your-eyebrows-off bitter. My mother drank it with relish. The rest of us drank it when we needed to. We didn't know any other possibilities existed.

But, in the late 1970s, in Kansas, Jer and I discovered Peet's mail-order whole-bean coffee from San Francisco. Peet's was a revelation, a thousand miles away and a thousand degrees of flavor from Folgers bought at Emporia's Albertsons.

Initially we ordered our Peet's ready-ground, and we made the elixir with our Melitta pour-over coffee set, cream-colored base, and filter holder. I learned to use three times the amount of coffee my mother used, hang the cost. Later, we acquired a bright red coffee grinder and went to whole beans; fresh ground was revelatory. The Melitta carafe was too small, so over the years we bought and broke a variety of bigger carafes. When we moved to Portland, we found a gold filter, a $20 extravagance, to replace the papers inside the ceramic holder. The original Melitta holder was broken in 2019. The current carafe is stainless steel, and its filter holder is plastic.

So, for 40 or so years, we have made coffee by grinding the beans in the red grinder that spews grounds over the counter, after which we decant the fresh grounds into the gold filter. The filter is then placed on top the stainless-steel carafe, where it lists slightly because the carafe top is not flat. Then we pour boiling water through the ground beans. The smell is glorious. The coffee wonderful.

And the process is fraught.

The grinder always makes a mess on the top of the counter.
I have caught the hot carafe with the sleeve of my nightgown
and dropped the whole shebang on the floor. Arthritis in
my wrists and thumbs and a rotator cuff injury to my right
shoulder has made pouring the full pots of hot water dangerous.

But it was looking at Roz Chast's drawings of her mother's
worn and patched hot pads that made me realize we were at
a new stage of development. We needed to buy an automatic
coffee maker.

It turns out that automatic coffee makers have changed since
1964. They now turn themselves on at pre-programmed
times. They have burrs that grind the whole beans. They
have modes for coffee strength and amounts of water. The
coffee maker I found had glowing reviews. *Wirecutter* called it
"superb;" the coffee was touted as swoon-worthy.

And so, the beautiful monster came yesterday in a big box
with a fat shiny book of instructions. I spent a couple
hours at the dining room table reading about set-up. Later,
I watched YouTube videos, listening to earnest engineering
types, explaining ponderously. No music.

This morning, we rearranged the kitchen to set it up. I programmed the auto-brew function. I tested the on-off switch.
I cleaned it with water and vinegar to rid it of residual dust.
I refilled the water reservoir to the red line, set the strength
dial to hair-on-your-chest mode, and dropped the first batch
of Peet's beans into the top container. I put the lid on the
bean holder and pushed the green auto button, which will
awaken the system at the prescribed time. Tomorrow, the
beans will slide into the grinder as auto-instructed.

By the time I finished, Jer had ground our Peet's beans in the red grinder—which let loose its spray of fine roast onto the counter. He had boiled water in the hot pot, set up the carafe, and put the fresh ground beans into the gold filter. The water was poured over the ground beans and not onto the floor, it dripped condescendingly into the carafe, and we had our morning coffee.

Tomorrow morning, god willin' and the crick don't rise, we'll arise to auto-ground-and-brewed, wonderful-smelling, West Coast elitist delight.

And so, an old person's project, a new acquisition to pierce my morning fog. Thank you, Roz Chast! Not dead yet.

Mama

July 2022

The new coffee maker, now a couple of years old, still works its magic; every morning it fills the kitchen with fresh-ground bean fragrance and calls me from my bed. And the coffee is still better than any we ever made under the old system. After 56 years, we successfully took on a new project. Not dead yet.

January 20, 2020
On Not Complaining

Dear Jan,

Five years ago, almost six now, I made a stout rule about getting old: "No conversations about bad health!!" No, no, no! We will not (I said) spend the last years of our lives rehearsing each other's meds and back pains, arthritis and prostates and knee surgeries. No.

But then, of course, I modified my stance. I do this quite a bit—make a no-nonsense, non-nuanced statement, and then back off.

It turns out that, like most theoretical absolutes in life, there are in actual practice, gray areas. It's sliding scale, it all depends on context, and ultimately whether it's morning, noon, or night, and whether I have had a bit of mutton that's given me indigestion.

As you see, this is not a simple notion—that old people shouldn't complain.

But it is a fun question to mull over.

I have a bit of trouble with one friend who invariably says that she knows that she shouldn't complain, that I have forbidden it, and that since she's sitting in my studio, she should obey my (she silently adds—ridiculous) rules, but really, her feet, oh her feet, oh oh oh.

I have then to decide, do I admit that in some circumstances complaining is not only permitted but essential? And try to get her to see that choices can be made about what to complain about?

Or, do I chime in and tell her about my feet, which are so painful by the end of the day that I don't want to cook dinner (although that's a bad complaint, because this friend knows I never want to cook dinner). This is not to mention that my calves ache after 7,000 steps and they are too tight but when I do the calf stretch exercises they really hurt, and that I can't, anymore, follow calf stretches with the thigh stretches (done by folding the lower leg up behind oneself and hanging onto the ankle to stretch the front of the thigh). Oh no, I can't do that, because it pulls on my bad knee and tweaks it so I can't walk on it for some minutes afterward and of course, it—the knee, I mean—aches for the rest of the day and into the night until I fall asleep.

Falling asleep isn't easy because of my vertigo and the itching, *almost* unbearable—I don't pass out, so it's bearable—around my neck and under my breasts and on my back.

The problem, which I now see quite clearly, is that one complaint leads to another, and, if there are two of you (and it's no fun complaining to oneself alone) there's a kind of competition about which complaint is worse. Imagine if there are three of us.

So, having a rule about no complaints, and then, just maybe, allowing a small whine to creep into the conversation, is how it works. The subheads which follow are the interesting parts. I say, "No Complaining"—and then gently probe the subheadings: cancer? Perhaps a bit of empathy. Knee replacement? Murmuring and clucking.

It is probably useful that my personality is seen as forceful and these non-conversations start in my space, my studio. That being the case, I get to decide what the rules are, and then, merrily, as the rule maker, I get to break them.

And with that, I'll admit, that I allow myself to complain. How else will you know that I was really, really brave all these years and only complained when it was really, really bad? I'm thinking the obituary and talk at my cremation, of course. Right now, the reason to hold the complaints down is that even my own are dreadfully boring if they go on for more than 37 seconds. So perhaps that will be my new rule: complaints can be made but must conclude within 37 seconds.

GO.

Yer silly mama,
June

May 12, 2020
A Walk in the Rain

Dear Jan,

In the middle of the pandemic, the neighborhood remained blooming as ever.

Today I walked a different route around the neighborhood; I tromped up pot-holed Flanders Street along the Brainard graveyard. The headstones inside the cemetery are erratically spaced, not gridded. Smack in the middle of the weathered memorials is a perfectly symmetrical apple tree. It pops up in bloom, pink-white, in the spring and in October drops its gold-yellow leaves in a perfect circle. Brainard Cemetery is one of those hidden places, known to its neighbors and unnoticed by almost everyone else.

Across from the cemetery, at the corner, is a large house, in need of paint—a house that I've walked by before but never really noticed. Today I saw that the residents had built eight raised veggie-beds using old lumber and cement blocks in the big side yard across from the graveyard. The planting beds were placed ungeometrically among thick, bent-over trees and unpruned shrubs. One of the trees reminded me of the tree we stole cherries from in Pine Station—a smooth-barked cherry, perhaps the Queen Ann variety, with thick side branches.

The raised beds were in various stages of growth; my favorite was full of strawberries, just past bloom, starting to set. Abandoned toys, aluminum lawn chairs, a listing metal table, as well as miscellaneous household tools were strewn about. A rope swing hung crookedly from a cherry limb.

Among the other stuff in the yard was a doll—a big doll, with a yellow raincoat and boots and blonde hair, that suddenly moved and reached out and wrinkled its fingers at me. It was a little kid, another growing thing, spring rain dripping from its slicker, its form almost eclipsed by the grass and rhubarb and weeds.

I turned the corner, walking past the front of the house, as the small girl went toward a shed, moving past the front door. More raised beds appeared, and then chickens, ranging about in their own fenced space, protected from visiting cats and coyotes. The chickens clucked, the papa of small child warily acknowledged my smile, and the small child, now investigating a rock on the front walk, stood up unsteadily, regained her balance, and wrinkled her fingers at me again.

All this was disorderly, unsuburban, full of messy life. Much like the cemetery, come to think of it, where the tombstones defied geometry.

I walked on in the rain.

Hugs,
Mama

Alert readers will note that I go from January to May to December with few reports about the neighborhood. Notes about those in-between days—pandemic, surgeries, insurrection—will be found elsewhere in this book. This section focuses on dailiness, how we live as middlin' elders, in the immediacy of the quotidian.

December 6, 2020
Sightings

Dear Jan,

After fussing with writing today, I found myself needing to clear my head. So, Jer and I meandered around the neighborhood. We started out on our usual route—across the suburban geography of the ridge (checking out the flags at the Trumpist house, reinstated after the election), through the public right-of-way and unofficial dog park that bisects the two Christian school campuses, across Burnside, and a zigzag through the flat residential neighborhood to Stark Street.

Standing in a green-strip above Burnside, a mama and a pink-coated three-year-old on a tricycle were looking at the traffic. As we went by them, the kid gabbled at us, waving her arms above her trike handles, laughing and gesturing at the cars, totally undecipherable. Her mom, seeing our bemusement, said that the little girl had just seen a tree on top of a car. It had turned her world upside down. The tricyclist continued to chatter, still undecipherable. Smiling, we agreed with her and walked on, and then we understood—a tree, especially a Christmas tree, strapped to a car! It has to be talked about, shouted about, pointed out so no one misses it. For a three-year-old, it is a marvel. As it should be for 78-year-olds.

On our way back home, we greeted the chickens, LaVerne, Patty, and Maxene, and turned the corner to go back up 86th. There, across the street, we saw that same little girl, gazing with astonishment at the collection of blown-up Christmas icons—Mickey Mouse with a Santa hat, Rudolph, nose glowing, an elf, whose behind stuck out of Santa's workshop. Mama was chatting with the homeowner, a woman we've often greeted and whose yard decor has always made us grin. She waved at us, little pink girl turned and gabbled a bunch of indecipherable tales, her arms flailing to get us to look at the balloon-crammed front yard. Mama waved also. A walker coming toward us smiled and said "Nice day! Not raining!" and we strolled on home.

The astounding shapes within our ordinary day.

Love you,
Mama

I come from a family of storytellers, where after-dinner coffee was pushed aside and laughter began. My original family used stories to take care of emotional issues, to put hurt into humorous context; they told stories to describe their days, so we all could share funny, poignant or rueful events. The stories were self-deprecating and had their roots and formatting in depression-era evenings—a tradition carried on at least through the 1980s. Back in north-central Pennsylvania, they may still continue to this day. And here, 3,000 miles away, I find myself continuing the tradition.

Stories, it turns out, are ways to shape the mist of experience. And experience itself, written down, becomes shaped, sometimes in spite of itself.

December 20, 2020
Jingle, Jangle

Dear Jan,

Here it is, the Sunday before Christmas, with carols from the All Classical station providing an undemanding background. Sometimes I hum along.

Our Squeave, the two-foot high Christmas squirrel/beaver that Janet Lunde sent us on a silly impulse has been sent into hiding. When Squeave is set on its perch, the wind picks it up and tumbles it down the driveway. So we've had to hunker it under the Japanese aralia. The other studio Christmas lights are bright but uninteresting. The dangling icicles of the Salings are much more festive.

The Graves, two doors down, have used twinkling lamps to gussy up their rhodies and azaleas. Kyle and Jenna next door don't have any outdoor lights—too busy with the two children and two jobs, perhaps. And further south on 85th, there are no lights at Mark's nor at the desolate house next to his, where we think the owner was caught out of town at the beginning of the pandemic.

At the front of the house, on 86th Avenue, there is more color. Our house has a modest strand of colored bulbs wound around the front porch railing. Next door, the Weatherbys' house is full of light, twinkles amid their flowerpots and hedges and up their spent vines across the front porch. Donna and Angie, the 40-year-olds across from us, have colored lights hung in swags along their front gutters. Next to them,

Mike and Linda's two-story cottage provides a good canvas for Christmas brightness.

The kids at the Christian school on our walking route have also been decorating for Christmas. Along the grassy right of way that divides the two campuses, as well as within the courtyards of the buildings, they've made wire figures, about three feet tall, which they decorate with hats and eyes and noses—mild-climate snowmen. I like imagining the students working in groups, deciding how to shape the wire to make the form, how to attach it to the stakes that stabilize it, where to find the greenery to hide the wire, and then, running off to locate hats and gloves and carrots to make faces for the dwarf-green figures.

And so, as we walk in the dim gray noon light, we take cheer from the yards where the puffed-up and beaming cartoon figures elbow each other for room. We smile at the fake gifts piled in front of the wire reindeer. And we are delighted to see the painted plywood cow has its seasonal Santa hat, dangling in front of its nose. We check to see who put up lights this year and who didn't. We note which houses sit empty, waiting for their owners to return from pandemic exile. We pay attention, because it is time for a seasonal tallying, a kind of kinwork.

Cheers and hugs, m'dear. We hope your lights are good and bright this year,

Mama

It was a bitter-sweet Christmas, determinedly cheery in the middle of the national crises—the pandemic unabated but with maybe a vaccine coming into being; an ex-president who wanted to become emperor for life and was using all the means he could command—legal, illegal, bullying, threatening, cajoling—to do so; another year on the way that would hold who knew what.

And Christmas carols were being sung, lights were being hung, small children stood with wide eyes, seeing the unthinkable, and neighborhoods held their breaths, hoping for a better season, a reasonably decent time, to come with the new year.

December 31, 2020
New Year's Eve Day

Dear Jan,

I was pleased to see you writing on Facebook about your "Season of Merriment." You have not inherited my anxiety and resentment about the period from Thanksgiving to January first. That's a relief.

Last night, caught in my own tiresome emotions, I dreamed I held a cylindrical container of liquid, trying to release a tiny mouse, trying again and again to pour it out so the mouse could run away. In my dream, I was unable to let the trapped creature go. I guess, like the mouse, I am not to escape my own emotional hangover.

However, reading about your cheerfulness and getting outside and looking at the world cheers me up. On today's meander, a 30-something skateboarder rolled by with a brindle dog on a leash. The dog, barely out of puppyhood, was indifferent to the skateboarder's ride straight down the street. The pup investigated each tree, every slab of grass parking, all the dead coreopsis and blackberry jumbles. As he did so, the leash tangled, but the pup dashed on ahead, until checked, of a sudden, by the restraint. Then he would stop and sniff a curb, go sideways when the skateboard moved forward, and take off again, a clown show of delight. His person was equally charmed; he laughed when the pup took a sudden leap sideways, upending the skateboard, and frightening a digging squirrel.

At busy Burnside, a mama and two children waited to cross. A van barreled down the street, shook itself, and came to a noisy stop. It sat idling noisily but patiently, while the little family gathered up its courage, checked both ways, again for moving cars and then checked again just to be sure, and finally meandered (the children) while being urged (by mama) to "move-along and let the nice driver go by."

The kids waved at me and went on up 85th, so for a long minute, I got to admire the little girl's outfit as they walked away. She had a purple-pink-striped ski hat with pompom ears. Her coat was hot pink, covered with multi-colored flowers. It was large on her, coming down the top of her boots. The coat looked new. I imagined that she had worn it to bed every night since Christmas.

The three of them wandered slowly up the street. I followed, even slower, waving to Gavin who was pulling in his trash bins from the curb. I checked the poetry box at the house next door—empty—and told myself that I should fill it up with a New Year's poem.

And by the time I got to the studio, even my memories of resentment had flown away into the brisk wind. I vacuumed some dust mice from behind the printer stand and shook the bathroom rug. Then I moved a piece of furniture, just to have a bit of a change, and settled into my computer, to see what was up.

So happy Merriment Day, my love. Your birthday always reminds me how tidily and neatly you arrived and how cheery and good you always have been. And so I'm thinking that perhaps I have escaped another year's slosh of old tired holiday anxieties. Away with them and on to the New Year.

Hugs,
Mama

February 11, 2021
What's In a Word?

Dear Jan,

I have been accused, correctly perhaps, of using the word "desultory" a bit too often. But what's not to love about "desultory"—a state of being as well as the word itself?

Desultory, a blissful mindlessness, is described by a word that slips away from the mouth like the eyes slide over the moss at the wet winter's edge. Mouthing "desultory" is like wandering around in one's nightgown, hot coffee in a round red cup, picking up last week's *New Yorker* and then dropping it back on the couch.

To be clear, when I say "desultory," I do not mean casual, or halfhearted, or lukewarm, or cursory. This is not about being dilatory, although that's a good word too. Nor is it about idleness or lackadaisicallity or fecklessness.

Oh no: desultory means intentionally blank. Being desultory involves aimless, haphazard, random, and fitful moments, but is more than just that. It is a marked indefiniteness, a purposeful lack of purpose.

Now dilatory is a pretty good synonym but lacks the sleepy sound of the "s." And "idleness" while it does have those delicious "d" and "s"s, it lacks the wussy goal-lessness of desultory. And certainly "feckless," is much too thumping with its "f" and "k."

When I describe my day as desultory, I am speaking of an immersion into blank movement that goes nowhere and returns from nowhere. It's an action not connected with any notions, goals, or objects (I refer you again to that half-opened *New Yorker* in the folds of the tossed throw on the couch next to last week's Sunday *Oregonian* and a few crumbs of potato chips). And as "desultory" moves through the mouth, like a roll of soft smoke with a "d" slithering into the hiss of the "s" and the gentle ululation of "u" falling from the twinkle of the "t" and the sigh of the "y"—well, what's not to love about it?

What's not to love about a day in which the nose wrinkles as the coffeepot gurgles? A book about something gets picked up and put down, and the clock ticks. A sock is dangled aloft, waiting to be pulled onto a foot, while the mind moves past the dripping faucet.

There's a tenderness in the picking up and laying down of a dusty knickknack. The air is warm and soft, the clothes cuddle and soothe, the tree outside has fine curved limbs, the sky is various but doesn't care.

The chair envelopes the body, the book lies in the lap, the eyes close slowly. What's not to love about being desultory, having a desultory day, moving desultorily through the house, and loving all things—in a desultory way.

Your smiling,
Mama

February 13, 2021
Hoar Frost February

Dear Jan,

We just experienced our January thaw, a long one this year, fooling me into thinking that spring had sprung.

Spring has been postponed.

Yesterday rain and sleet blew in from the Columbia Gorge, blasted our east Portland knoll, and then slithered down to the Willamette River and south into the valley. By the time it was sleeting in Salem, it was snowing—or rather, bouncing ice—here. Then came the wind and the real snow—blizzard-type snow—lightweight, tiny flakes, blowing sideways. The wind pushed up the snow eddies into piles, and by the time we got up this morning, the drifted mounds were two feet and more.

It's fun to watch the snow fold and drift off the roofs, like great clouds of mist. The steps to the studio are completely obliterated while parts of the deck are almost bare. Geppetto the cat has not been seen this morning; we think he's staying inside, but he may just be tunneling through drifts.

I got up early, quietly excited about the scene outside. The trees were bending and tossing as the wind caught them— the big Doug fir behind the studio is good for its drama.

As I sat watching the early morning out the library window, the wind ceased, and the world stilled. Hoarfrost started accumulating, slowly emerging on the lilacs by the window, on the bushy fir limbs, on the persimmon and each tiny maple twig.

Hoarfrost consists of tiny crystals, accumulating slowly, individually, clinging onto the lines of branches and each other. The ice-diamonds reflect the glowing light from each of their beveled edges and contours. At the same time, the branches and grasses remain washes of black ink.

Once or twice I have seen hoarfrost after it completed its coverage, each branch in a grove of shimmering trees. But I never saw hoarfrost *growing*, slowly, air turning to sparkled light on twigs and branches, increasing in density until the whole world is covered in glass. I held my breath, feeling that a wisp of air could bring it all crashing down. It accumulated, thickened, brightened, shone until I had to squint: it was everywhere and everything. It held there, and I had to breathe and yet it still held. And then the ice shivered and started to slide.

The crystalline light dropped into more ordinary moistness, and the trees became sharp lines against a gray world. Branches re-emerged. The world returned to shrubs and snow, odd sticks emerging from the snowdrifts, pleasant mounds punctuated by the sides of walls and pots. Very nice. Very arty. But not magic.

Yer Ma,
June

February 14, 2021
The Light of Snow

Dear Jan,

Describing light is like describing taste. It's much easier to say, "oh, come on over and I'll show you!"

Portland has gotten 10 official inches of blowing snow, preceded by ice and followed by rain and ice with more snow, rain, ice to come. But it's not the snow that gathers me in today. It's the light.

Do you remember how we used to sit in winter twilight, first in Wyoming and then in Kansas? The snow would contain the light after the sky darkened, and a hush—a suspension—gave us a sense of simple monolithic being. Alas, in most Portland winters, there are few suspended twilights. The snow, when there is snow, mingles with earthy things—grasses and dead foliage, shrubbery and rhodies—making it a mixed tone, without its own light. Portland snows, ordinarily, don't light up the world.

This snow is not ordinary. This is a Kansas snow.

The light is bright from the ground up. The sky has some luminosity, with the sun behind the lowering clouds, but it's the snowed-in earth that is breath-expanding. The snow stretches out. It's all of single undifferentiated expanse—roofs, soil, grass, yucca plants, and concrete steps—all folded into the whites of snowdrifts.

And then, as I continue to gaze out the window, the trees come into focus. They are coated, not the daintiness of hoarfrost but the sturdiness of ice. Each twig and bud is rounded in semi-transparency, underneath which the branch shows gray. The ice catches the snow-light, shimmering and skidding around the adjoining branches. The light on the mounds of ground snow forms the faintest of grays and blues and purples, making a world both singular and various, containing the tips of iris and muffled cat prints and twigs broken from ice-laden trees.

Of course, we expect to lose our power later today. Limbs will break and trees will come down and snowplows will despair, and powerline workers will brave the elements. But that's a human story. This morning's story is nature's. The light, single and various, is all there is.

Hugs,
Mama

March 3, 2021
Neighboring Season

Dear Jan,

It's a gorgeous spring day. A wintry mix of rain and sleet and snow is scheduled in a few days; for now, we must bask.

Light lingers into the evening, and so we walk after the nap and a cup of tea. Because the weather is so enticing, everyone else comes out. It's neighboring season.

We were a couple of blocks from home, up Everett Street, where there are no sidewalks, when a slow-moving sedan came around the corner from 90th Avenue. We moved over to the side to let it by, but halfway around the corner, the car rolled to a stop. I glanced over and the window swished down.

A tiny woman was driving. She was masked against the Covid virus and had a transparent plastic bandana over her short, pink-bowed ponytail. She said something, clearly a question. I couldn't make out what she wanted (damned masks) and stepped closer to the car, which was still sitting cattycornered across the intersection:

"Pardon?"

"Are you the people who live behind me?" she asked.

I don't know this particular section of the neighborhood very well, but I couldn't think that the row of houses behind us, with all the kids and cats and dogs, had her in it.

As I puzzled, she clarified. "I live just down there at the corner."

So I knew we didn't live behind her, and I said so, trying to sound regretful. I was a bit worried. She *was* stopped in the middle of the intersection.

"I just wanted to tell you that if you were those people who lived behind me—they moved out a while back and left three cats—and I just wanted to tell them about their cat."

I nodded, thinking happily that, oh yes, we were in the middle of neighboring season.

"The big black one. I'm Darlene, by the way, and that big black cat, I just discovered, that that big black cat likes country music. Have you ever heard of such a thing?"

"Oh," I said, "oh, that's wonderful. We once had a cat that liked opera!"

"Is that so?" She seemed to be beaming behind her mask. "Well, I never heard of a cat who liked music. This one, she just sits in front of my speakers and listens when I play Johnny Cash." The car was still sitting halfway around the corner in the middle of the intersection.

"I just got back from taking lemonade and coffee to the homeless," she continued, nodding to some empty bags on the seat beside her. "It was a good day for them—they can get out and be warm and dry, you know."

I said that that was a really good thing.

"Well, you know, they are living, living in their cars and trailers, but still it's really cold and nasty sometimes."

"Thank you for helping them," I said.

She waved her hand at me, brushing away thanks. And then toodled, "Bye-bye" and drove, very slowly, down the street, turning at the house at the corner, guiding her sedan into the unpaved gravel.

So now we know a bit about Darlene, even maybe where she lives. Another note for the refrigerator: Darlene, black cat, brick house, gravel street. We'll remember to check out her drooping lilies as we walk by next time. We'll look for that black cat.

Mama

II

ELDERHOOD AND ITS REVELATIONS

There are years that ask questions and years that answer.
—Zora Neale Hurston

June 7, 2019
Gnarly Fallen Parts

Dear Jan,

The May 2019 *Smithsonian Magazine* features Henrik Saxgren's photo of an elderly Greenland hunter. The hunter is holding a cigarette between his first finger and his pinkie. He had lost the two middle fingers to frostbite, years before.

The hunter says about his missing fingers: "There is little meaning in making a fuss. There is nothing else to do but to say good-by to the lost body part and continue your life with what parts are left."

Jer and I often talk about aging as the time when "parts fall off." The Greenland hunter and Jer share a stoicism about the body—as time encroaches, our physical parts misbehave, losing their fluidity. "Things fall off" stands for a whole class of events, like arthritis in the knees and thumbs, thinning skin that bruises, teeth that feel loose in their sockets, and cold feet whose bite starts in the bone. Brown spots ("age spots") appear, and as gravity works its forces, fat cheeks sag, and round faces become square and, unwittingly, sour looking. I speak, my dear, of myself.

Facing the physical fact of aging is difficult because, even with exercise and careful training, you are not going to come out the other side better, more shapely, stronger. Nope, at best you will sit on a plateau until something else falls off. Parts that fall off in our elderhood often can't be picked up and put back on. And, because the falling off of parts is ubiquitous, universal, inevitable, and generally irreversible: "there is little meaning in making a fuss."

Ursula Le Guin is pretty frank about the aging body: "For old people," she says, "beauty doesn't come free with the hormones, the way it does for the young. It has more to do with bones. It has to do with who the person is. More and more clearly it has to do with what shines through those gnarly faces and bodies."

She is clear that that which "shines through" doesn't fall off or turn gnarly. It could even grow and shine more brightly. I mostly agree with Le Guin, although some of us don't have her bones to resist the pull of gravity. However, I rather like being "gnarly" rather than just wrinkled. Wrinkled is what I am, but gnarly is what I claim. We have grown out of our hormones, and there's little meaning in making a fuss.

Mama

June 8, 2019
Parts Falling Off, Continued

Dear Jan,

I chuckled as I wrote "Continued" above. It's the one certainty, you know—that our parts will continue to fall off, even after we lie moldering in our graves.

Jer and I were cozy in our respective chairs last evening, talking about our various ailments, when I opined that there was "little meaning in making a fuss."

"Well," he said, grinning at me, he would change "little meaning" to "little use." Or even, "little point" in making a fuss.

"Oh no," I said, taking up the challenge. "'Little meaning' is perfect."

He raised his eyebrows.

"Little meaning in making a fuss," I opined, is more interesting than "little use or point," because what meaning is there in *fussing?* All living things have parts that eventually fall off. Fussing about this just takes up time, and our time is getting short. Fusses aren't meaningful. Making a fuss about one's aging processes is an indulgence; the pain of others, in war or refugee camps or domestic traumas, can be so much greater. There's little meaning in our own small fusses.

"Ah," Jer said, "but what about 'Death is the mother of beauty?'" (my favorite quote from Wallace Stevens' "Sunday Morning").

We know that making a fuss could bring us face to face with an inevitable future and so, Stevens said, we *must* treasure the beauty that exists right now. Shouldn't knowing that nothing gold can stay make us treasure the moments that exist?

So we sat, silent for a minute, thinking about how precious the remaining teeth and knees are, now that some are falling off.

And then, he added, another use of fuss-making is that people commiserate and bring you chocolate drinks.

Ah, I said, there's the rub. There's little use in making a fuss because, ultimately, no one can soothe the agues of aging. Even warm drinks and soothing clucks don't bring back the lost fingers or limber knees.

And caregivers have their own parts that ache and come to mishaps. They can't always be providing comfort; they need to make their own fusses. And then, in turn, we have to listen and commiserate and try not to discuss all our own ailments, at least not at that minute.

Of course, fusser and commiserator could join in raising our glasses to the efficiency of organic life; ultimately our parts join those who have gone before in an eternal recycling— ashes to ashes, dust to dust, flesh to compost to daisies and green beans. We could possibly use our fusses to comprehend our place in the scheme of things.

We both agreed, however, that when that front tooth falls out, one's common humanity is beside the point. So, no meaning? no use? no point? in making a fuss?

Adam Gopnik, in *The New Yorker* says perhaps the way to age would be to remain middle-aged (about 50 or so) into our 90s—and then die. Which reminded us both that years ago, in our 50s and 60s, we clambered over rocks and stayed up until 2 AM, and were eloquent and easy with words and names. Our toes didn't hurt when the sheets were too tight; our teeth didn't rattle when we bit into apples.

But we have not stayed middle-aged in our elderhood. We are old, and, right now, there's little use, point, or meaning in making a fuss. I have conceded.

However, and Jer nods, perhaps another notion would suffice. Rather than debate meaning, point, and usefulness, I could just grumble.

"Grumbling," I said (Jer was grinning at me) " 'grumbling' is *not* making a fuss. When things fall off, no matter how softly they thud, I will just grumble."

Hugs,
Mama

Jer is my spouse of 59 years, and we find great comfort in exposing our itches and foibles to each other. He puts up with my "argufying" and "contrariwise-ness" and I put up with his careful accounting and inability to know when to water the plants. We both love silly words, particularly if they are almost obsolete ("ague" is a case in point). We are a mutual admiration society, smoothed and fitted through many years of rubbing along together. He's 40 pounds lighter than I am, and much better at math. I am more gregarious and better at growing things. He's bald, and I have wild hippie hair. But even in our complementing selves, we have taken on something of each other's character. We grin at our mutual foibles, hang onto each other when crossing the boulevards of our neighborhood, and issue each other warnings about tripping hazards. It's all good, even when we disagree about making a fuss.

June 1, 2019
On Writing in Your Undies

Dear Jan,

I'm writing to you, dressed only in my undies. This disclosure makes me snigger, because I generally don't, in my elderhood, discuss my naked or near-naked body. But mostly I giggle because it's great fun, at age 77, to write in one's undies.

I haven't wandered, half-dressed, around the house for years. When I was in good shape, post-marathon 50s, I was inclined to stride through the house, not giving a damn about who might glimpse me through the windows. Now, however, my body no longer feels free and open to striding; I find its lumps and bumps and sags disconcerting; I like them covered by jeans and turtleneck shirts. My back hunches when I'm tired, my ankles swell in the heat. Thinking of wandering nearly naked, even with the blinds firmly drawn, is fairly horrifying. However, here, in my upstairs attic room, sitting at my computer, knees sweating and the temperature hovering around 90, I have shucked my clothes. I am writing in my undies.

At 90 degrees in the privacy of my attic hideaway—who cares? No one can see me, up under the eaves. Without a mirror I don't even see myself.

Of course, the question of "what undies" could crop up, so let me explain.

No bra among these undies, but then I haven't worn a bra since the '60s. Which is not quite true, but makes a good story. I was for years an under-endowed woman, so wearing a bra was pretty much beside the point. And after I turned 60 and my shape changed, who cared anyway, even if the weight gained gave me more flesh to contain. So, only panties, or scanties, or whatever we call them these days. Panties, it turns out, are useful for me, even at age 77.

And saying this makes me grin. So I'm happy, sitting in the heat and the cool light of my attic lair, writing in my undies.

However, I will sign this more formally, just to signal that I'm now back in normal disguises—turtleneck, blue jeans, respectable aged citizen once again.

So,
June O. Underwood

Confessions of this sort can make people squirm; elderhood is best observed from a distance, fully clothed, where cooing over the cute elders gives the youngers a sense of superiority. Even one's beloveds might say "Grand-mère, too much information!"

OK, I get it. But this is how it is, and, trust me, you too may turn into an elder one day. I'm writing to examine how one (this one, me) elder moves around her space, how it might differ from how she navigated life in her adulthood, what feelings these private changes bring about, and what makes her laugh among the lumps and wrinkles. That's all. That's not too much information, is it?

June 19, 2019
Some Wisdom

Dear Jan,

I have complained that the notion of "wisdom" in elderhood is bunkum.

I stand corrected. Yesterday I acquired some wisdom.

I was at the dentist, with a sharp toothache that I had had, although not so sharp, for some days, maybe some weeks. The assistant, a gentle young soul in her mid-30s, reproached me for not coming in sooner. I said that we had just concluded a four-day holiday in which "sooner" was not, except in the case of high fevers with hallucinations, really an option.

She pointed out that I had told her I had been having symptoms, a sharp pain in that tooth (but only, I said, when I ate nuts or chewed on ice) for a couple of weeks. I allowed as how (both of us being conversational and non-confrontational) that sometimes those sharp pains go away; the nerve calms down all by itself, making nothing but a tiny fuss for a couple of days. Oh, she said, but you should have come in.

This conversation went on for a while, and then the dentist appeared. The assistant told her boss that she had reminded me that I should have come in earlier. The dentist, fixing a drill into her machine, said nothing. I said I thought the pain might disappear and save them the trouble of telling me that the pain might disappear. The young thing said, no, it was always better to come in.

A zealous young thing, I thought to myself. She's read all the manuals.

And then the dentist, herself verging on 60, leaned over and stage-whispered to me: "I would have done the same thing."

So—the wisdom of the elder is that sometimes the pain goes away without paying any attention to it.

And sometimes it doesn't.

In this case, I need a root canal. The pain is not going to go away.

Yer Mom

June 20, 2019
Mullings on an Aging Ash Tree

Dear Jan,

I am sitting on our front porch, the little 'burb porch that we've tarted up with clematis and flowerpots, watching Jer trim dead bits from the big ash tree in the front parking. From time to time, my handwriting slips off the notebook page because I've been taken with a coughing fit. I caught Jer's head cold and I'm feeling poorly.

I mention the ailment to explain why I'm sitting around watching Jer work. I believe that when there's work to be done, we all should pitch in. It's a good principle because it gets things done. However, a coughing fit can interfere with efficiency. So I sit and watch.

Earlier I pruned the hedge, and then sat down on the porch to watch Jer take limbs off the old tree. I think: "I am watching the ash as it dies."

Having a cold brings out the maudlin in me.

The truth is that I can't see the old ash dying. But I can see signs of its diminishment, its scatter of dead limbs and unseasonably browned leaves. The tree is still full of its own sweet swishes, leaves that hang and sway to their own music, but its time is limited.

It's a beloved tree, one that the neighbors praise and pet. (Although one neighbor tells us, in a tough voice, that it's-a-beautiful-tree-but-not-worth-much-very-soft-wood--you-know-can't-last-long). When we moved here five years ago, the arborist told us it had about five years left, and Jer prunes the lower branches, hoping to preserve the tree's strength for another year or two.

The tree, meant to grow 40 or 50 feet high, had been topped by the previous owner. The top must have been dying—otherwise, why cut it—but we were dismayed by its maimed appearance. But there it was, and there we were, and we had a new house to set up and we soon grew very fond of its lumpish shape. And then it grew tall fronds of new branches from its wounds. It lived and looked good.

The tree's new foliage, wispy compared to the heavy trunk, reminds me of my quilted art work, in the 1990s and 2000s. At that time I was ill with vertigo and desperate for something besides illness to occupy myself. I read of the principles of art and design and learned to use a sewing machine. I was inefficient and erratic but liked the work and believed I would get better. I see now that I sprouted and ventured and pushed outward like those new willowy ash branches.

I grew more adept, getting better at the sewing and absorbing design principles. I began dyeing fabric and found myself enthralled with the colors of hand-dyed cloth. Sometimes I dyed greens, browns, blues, cerulean, indigo, forest greens, and terra rosa, that mingled or made lines against each other. As a child in Pennsylvania, I had played under lime-green foliage swaying against the blues of the sky. Art reintroduced me to these colors, and I watched them blending and bouncing off one another, like watching the ash tree stretch from its truncated self into the sky.

I have my own personal favorites from those hand-painted and dyed art works of the 2000s: *The Coming Dark* and the *Willard Women* series are all about family. *The Coming Dark*, with the blue iris and upright green leaves, floating on the black background, was finished shortly after Mom died. My mother loved iris. I think her inner life was much like my own, only she was quieter and less appreciated for it. Her Alzheimer's took that mind away, as the family, unthinkingly yet surely, had quelled it earlier.

The Willard Women series, done some years later, is about you, daughter Jan, and me, of course, but also about Mom— Mom, whose life had been truncated by circumstance, but who grew up and through and around the scars. *Mrs. Willard Waltzes with the Wisteria* has a painted and quilted figure dancing through a wisteria vine of arched fabrics, stitched in meandering, willowy lines.

***

And here in the present, as I watch from the porch, comes our neighbor, admiring Jer's handling of the long saw. The neighbor is telling him, once again, how the beautiful ash is a fast-growing but doomed tree. He looks up. And then back at the ground. I think he is getting ready to lose it, dismissing it before it breaks his heart.

Jer puts down the saw. He's done what he can. And my cough has subsided.

My mother, as her mind's grip on family and chores loosened, would sit and watch family, a swirl of toddlers and teenagers, fathers and siblings, chattering, sneaking food off the table, getting noses wiped. Now I watch Jer, pruning the tree. I wonder if the ash is watching us, Jer and me, observing us as it observed the others who came before us. Even the neighbor, I imagine, watches the tree—and us—from his front window.

Of course, time will overtake us all. Someday, someone else will sit on this porch and watch the neighborhood. We will have turned to dust, the tree will be gone to compost, the dour neighbor will be replaced by a younger person, all part of that cycle.

Much love,
Mama

" 'Burb"—a household designation, meaning old suburb like this one from 1949—not old enough to wring nostalgia, yet not young enough to be enticing, a 'burb constructed when houses were little boxes with four rooms and a bath, large yards and clean curbs. Now these boxes have grown higher and wider and deeper through additions, the yards have been in-filled with rhodies and trees, vegetable gardens, garages, granny dwellings, and other skinnier, houses. The streets have taken on individuality and charm, just as old people add their individual eccentricities to their accumulation of years.

And the old ash tree, a golden desert ash, still lives, eight years after we first saw its truncated top. It's a bit thinner all around and drops small branches onto the sidewalk with every breeze, but still alive. The arborist revised his estimate of the time it has left and has promised to come by every summer to see if it needs more TLC. Not Dead Yet, we all say.

June 27, 2019
Sagging Skin

Dear Jan,

I woke up this morning, stretched my toes and, still lying flat, sleepily reached toward the ceiling to work out the night stiffness. I reached into the light coming from the upper unshaded windows. It made luminous my upper arms; I saw golden color morphing into lavender in long ribbons of loosely attached flesh.

The colors smoothed themselves over and through my ridged, loose skin. In the light of the early bright sun, the long rows of wrinkles down my arms were purple and pink and salmon, tipped with gold. The lines and shadows were translucent and shimmered a bit as they streamed toward my shoulders. The flesh captured the light and refracted its colors, turning golden and lavender, with ribbony edges to show off curving flesh. It was shockingly beautiful.

Is this discovery of beauty "wisdom"? If so, it's the wisdom of happening upon something new, something that goes against all my thinking about my sagging skin. This was not the accumulated experience of fleshly delights but an entirely new and unexpected fleshly pleasure.

And I thought, waking a bit, that I was seeing a whole new world, a world in which sagging flesh was made miraculous. A new developmental stage of life indeed.

Hugs,
June

June 28, 2019
Revelation

Dear Jan,

Last evening at a chamber music concert, I was startled once again to realize that the way you feel may not be echoed by your looks. At my age, it's ridiculous to have the same revelation, over and over again. And yet, here I was.

We were at Reed College in a Chamber Music Northwest concert, sitting mid-way up the risers. The upper seats of the small auditorium allow us to see the musicians as they sweat and check in with sidelong glances at each other. The seats are cheaper, and our fellow seatmates interestingly dressed. Behind us last night was a young couple, enchanted with the program, delighted with the players, the range of music, other concert-goers, the whole scene. After each piece, they clapped enthusiastically, laughed and talked (with some sophistication) about what they had heard. I imagined they were students, attending to hear one of their beloved profs.

The program, featuring the clarinet, was mostly modern stuff, ragtime, jazz, blues, and a new composition called "Expeditionary Airmen, Three Day Pass," composed by Jeff Scott, a French horn player with the Amani Winds.

There was also some Mendelssohn, making use of the basset horn (look it up—we had to) which sounded new and fresh. The concert finished with a lied by Schubert about a sorrowful suiter. The lied, a lovelorn ballad, was sung by a long-skirted mezzo-soprano, all in black. The accompaniment was carried on by a jazz clarinetist in shirt sleeves and khakis. The formally dressed soprano stood tall and composed in front of the mic, making modest hand movements, moving only her voice through the florid embellishments and the undulating cadences. The jazz clarinetist, however, bent his body deep over his instrument, then pointed it skyward, wailing, as he conveyed the complaints of the lonely lover. The musical and visual differences illuminated two versions of an age-old story, two different musical instruments, two ways of wailing about love, the 19th century formality confronting a 20th century riff.

In short, it was a fine immersive evening. As we started to leave, we saw the young couple, still chuckling and gesturing, advancing through the crowd. They were deft and efficient and had long gone through the doors to the outside as Jer and I were still working our way out of our row of seats. My legs were stiff and wobbly from sitting so long, and I clutched at the stair railing, listening to the smiling comments of those moving down with us. I neared the bottom stairs as Jer, who had been swept along by the crowd, went ahead. The railing ceased to exist before the last two steps. I glanced at an elderly usher, who, seeing me hesitate, reached out and helped me down. I took his hand, stepped carefully, thanked him, and moved on.

And then I realized that the "elderly" usher I had seen was probably 15 years younger than I. He was seeing something very different from what I was envisioning. I was seeing myself, insofar as I was at all conscious of self, as this bouncy creature, full of music and delight. He saw a slow elderly woman, needing help to navigate the last few steps.

I went on to the lobby to find Jer. And out into the summery evening we went, an old couple, hitched to one another for stability, for *camaraderie* and for love.

Remember how you felt the first time a young guy jumped up to offer you his seat? Or worse, the first time an 18 year-old woman did the same? Or when you got the AARP offer in the mail? Well, at our age, the upwelling emotion is just the same—a bit funny, a bit eye opening, a bit revelatory.

Mama

June 29, 2019
Flow

Dear Jan,

In 2019, Adam Gopnik wrote a long article on aging in *The New Yorker*. It caught the attention of many of my aging friends, both elders and near-elders. Gopnik does what any *New Yorker* writer would do—he explores the new science and ideas, he interviews researchers and quotes them, he investigates both physical and mental tribulations of aging, and the available fixes.

However, he begins the article with what he assumes to be the normal process of moving beyond, say, 60 years of age. He describes it as "a series of lurches: eyes occlude, hearing dwindles, a hand trembles where it hadn't, a hip breaks—the usually hale and hearty doctor's murmur in the yearly check-up, *'There are some signs here that concern me.'*"

Gopnik was 63 when the article was published, and he was definitely worried about the future.

During his first foray into researching the article, at the Massachusetts Institute of Technology Age Lab, he is put into a simulated aging "costume." The material, nicknamed AGNES, makes him clumsy, "every small task becomes effortful." He has to think about reaching for the cup, about making his way clumsily across the room.

He says of moving around in the simulated aging suit: "Your emotional cast, as focused task piles on focused task, becomes one of annoyance; you acquire the same set-mouthed, unhappy, watchful look you see on certain elderly people on the subway. The concentration that each act requires disrupts the flow of life, which you suddenly become aware is the happiness of life, the ceaseless flow of simple action and responses, choices all made simultaneously and mostly without effort. Happiness is absorption, and absorption is the opposite of willful attention."

Of course, at 63, Gopnik is just on the verge of having to face elderhood.

One researcher puts it this way: "From zero to twenty-one is about eight thousand days. From twenty-one to midlife crisis is eight thousand days. From mid-forties to sixty-five—eight thousand days. Nowadays, if you make it to sixty-five you have a fifty-per-cent chance you'll make it to eighty-five. Another eight thousand days!"

Poor Adam Gopnik imagines these last 8,000 days as nothing but a series of lurches into horrors—bad eyes, bad ears, bad hands, bad hips, and sad doctors. He imagines that as an adult one is hale and hearty and then, as an elder, self-conscious and pissed off with one's every move. "The suit makes us aware not so much of the physical difficulties of old age, which can be manageable, but of the mental state disconcertingly associated with it—the price of age being perpetual aggravation."

I tend to sympathize with Gopnik, who imagines facing a long life with nothing but self-conscious inadequacies and "perpetual aggravation." But I want to reassure him:

It isn't all that bad.

Gopnik says we lose the "flow" of body movements and imagines that that will make us angry all the time.

A wise man once said, it isn't the pain, it's imagining the pain that is most debilitating.

I would nudge Mr. Gopnik with this.

Humans are incredibly adaptable.

In each age, we may come to points of dismay and fear, but we move beyond self-consciousness and enjoy the present— seeing a tattooed gent do an elegant turn on the skateboard, watching a couple of "kids" bounce down auditorium steps, or even finishing a fine article for a premiere magazine.

Look at me dance, I say to myself, as I stumble around the studio to a bit of Mozart.

And listen to Lear for a minute:

> "When thou dost ask me blessing, I'll kneel down
> And ask of thee forgiveness. So we'll live,
> And pray, and sing, and tell old tales, and laugh
> At gilded butterflies, and hear poor rogues
> Talk of court news, and we'll talk with them too –
> Who loses and who wins, who's in, who's out –

And take upon us the mystery of things
As if we were God's spies."

It's Gopnik who reminds us that we (the elders, with whom he is starting to think he may have something in common) may be "God's spies"; at the end of his article he puts on a brave face. Even so, he can imagine no kind old age; the best we can hope for is "a single American age, a kind of shared perpetual middleness, where we will dye our hair and take our pills and suddenly collapse in the midst of the dance. Right now, we live well, and then we don't live well, and then we die. The most that science seems to offer us is this: We'll live well, and then we'll die."

Somehow, this crabby ending—science being way behind our desires—is unworthy of such a fine thinker. Gopnik has written the quintessential "Oh my god I'm getting old and nothing can help me" essay. We love him because he writes so well and thinks so strongly. I hope he weighs in when he's an elder to let us know how it goes for the first half of the rest of his life.

In the meantime, I will continue to try to be the goddesses' spy, as Lear advised.

Hugs,
Mama

Is it a singularly American phenomenon—the fear of an old age spent waiting to die?

I am not equipped to answer—and apparently, neither is Gopnik, who says this is an "American age." There are rumors of other societies in which the elders are adored, pampered, and revered, but that is, of course, a view that is held by the youngers; it doesn't answer the question of the elders' inner knowledge of decay. And in many, perhaps most, societies outside prosperous countries with good health care, elders die be-

fore they spend much time aching and clumsy. So more research needs to be done. But personally, I can attest that while I ache with arthritis and lurch with clumsiness, I find new things and new ways to appreciate and enjoy. I never wanted to be middle-aged forever, although I would like to dance a bit better than I do now. But I never was a very good dancer, so there's that.

July 11, 2019
Alive, Alive Oh

Dear Jan,

I just reread Diana Athill's *Alive, Alive Oh*, published in 2015, one of two memoirs in which she celebrates her old age. At age 89, she wrote *Somewhere Near the End* (2009) and published *Alive, Alive Oh (2015)* at age 97. She published *A Florence Diary* in 2016, at age 98. And she lived until she was 101. Can't get much better testimony about aging than that.

Athill is a delight to read—matter-of-fact and funny. Also iconoclastic, tart-tongued, kind, never married, but with a series of lovers. In her last years at what she calls the nursing home (we now call it "independent living,") she finds herself giggling with another resident about falling asleep by remembering the sex they have had. Somehow that wasn't the idea of 90-year-olds that society touts.

The nursing home Athill lived in had manicured lawns, but the home's residents preferred cottage-style flowers and plantings. So she and a few others bought six roses to replace a clay-filled rubbish patch. A young able-bodied maintenance man dug holes for new bushes but had to leave before he could plant the roses. Athill and the others decide not to wait for him to return.

Three of the residents, two 94-year-olds and herself (three weeks before her 97th birthday), planted all six roses. One got into the hole; another pushed the wheelbarrow with the rose bushes close to the edge. Athill was in charge of compost and rose food. In the hole, the more nimble 94-year-old received the roses handed down by the two above and spread their roots. Athill tossed in fertilizer and compost, handful by handful. The two women hoisted the other back to solid ground, they tipped more compost out of a bucket, and then they scraped clay back into the hole. They pushed the soil down around the plants and stood back, shaky but delighted, admiring their work.

Athill says: "By the time we tottered back to our rooms we were too exhausted to speak, but we were very pleased with ourselves. One good thing about being physically incapable of doing almost anything is that if you manage to do even a little something, you feel great."

The roses, five months later, were developing buds. I suspect the women had a good time, bragging of their deed to the young fellow who dug the hole.

Good to have models. Good to have writers. Good to have roses.

July 12, 2019
This Quotidian

Dear Jan,

I just spent half-an-hour repotting plants and deadheading the hosta lilies. Half-an-hour is such a tiny amount of time. I thought it was at least 90 minutes. But no, it was 30.

And then I slumped in front of the computer, enveloped in a tired blankness. My eyes wandered without focusing. Finally I began to write, slowly, with lots of pauses, staring at the gardens.

In the olden days, when I was, like, 60, I could push myself and gain strength by doing a bit more each day. "Every day in every way, we can get better and better." That sort of thing. But I am now wise to my age. No physical excesses will make me stronger or decrease the flop of my ample bosoms. If I push myself, all that happens is that I am tireder. Maybe more contented, but definitely more tired. My legs start to wobble, my desire to snip one more flopping flower head wanes. I want some water, I want to sit down, I want to stop thinking about the next garden chore.

That's an effect of aging.

I know that doing more is never going to make me more strong. The spirit may be willing, but the flesh has changed, sunk into those irreversible ridges of skin. I think that I have accepted the change, become mellower, but I still have moments when I think I must push through the exhaustion and pull more weeds. And then I stand up and my back sends its warning pains, and my brain goes wispy. And I know it's time to quit.

As all the newspapers report, it's important for us elders to move. The reminder to stand up every half hour isn't a bad thing. It's just that getting up every half hour isn't ever going to make getting up easier. It is what it is, and at least for a while, that's the way it will remain. Or it will decline, by micro-inches, until one day, getting up requires help from the chair arms. Or the caregiver.

After 30 minutes of gardening, the body needs to sit down, to rest, to have a cup of tea, to celebrate the hosta and the potted plant on the front steps. Then one's body (one being me, of course) will go inside and read a bit and have some lunch, or meander slowly to Monti's for the cup of coffee. No more upgrades—just hanging onto the current status. No, it's not what I thought would happen when I was 60, when I expected I could control the physical changes through exercise and willpower. I can no longer do that. So I have to celebrate the hostas and taste the tea and put aside as false lying nostalgia my notions about spading the other side of the yard. Actually it feels good to set that aside; Monti's for coffee is much better.

Hugs,
Mama

The ordinary life, our dailyness, the quotidian, is for the elders, as it is for toddlers, the basic stuff of our lives. The striving towards future goals becomes diminished or even vanished in our elderhood: we pay attention to what is directly in front of us, whether that's hosta lilies, arthritic thumbs and backs, or the morning NY Times. It's not a come-down, not a narrowing, however it may look to the middle-aged adult. Tennyson spoke of the tiny flower in the crannied wall, which, if he could understand it, would allow him to understand the whole of the universe. Thoreau says: "Nature will bear the closest inspection. She invites us to lay our eye level with her smallest leaf, and take an insect view of its plain." Voltaire, at the end of a long book examining the horrors of the human world, recommends that we cultivate our gardens. Gardens and flowers here are metaphors for the small daily forms and structures that we elders are immersed in. In elderhood, the grasping for something else goes away and our beings return to that childhood state of studying daily life.

To every age there is a season and a time for every purpose under heaven. Turn, turn, turn.

July 29, 2019
A Season Finale

Dear Jan,

Last night we went to the last concert of the Chamber Music's Summer Fest. We left full of music, Dvorak and Shubert, viola, violins, piano, cellos, providing tunes we now can't quite hum. The end of the season, but still filling us up.

As we left, I said "That was the best season we've ever had."

Jer agreed and added that maybe our five or so years of experience with these summer outings is what gives us this satisfaction. Certainly I'm a better concert-goer than I ever was, and I find greater pleasure in concerts than I ever did.

Why am I better at attending classical concerts? I don't hear better—age can make the violins screechy and the low notes harder to discern. Crowds are disconcerting, even orderly and courteous classical music crowds. And I'm opinionated about my classical music—Schubert can be boring, Mahler pompous, Wagner insufferable. And Mozart does tend to repeat his musical phrases *ad infinitum.*

Despite these kvetches, I have always liked music of all kinds. Mom bought discounted long-play classical records at the grocery store, and she and I listened to them for hours. Brother CJ and I sang country and western, Johnny Cash kinds of songs at school assemblies, and I loved '50s rock and roll and (Dad's influence) '40s crooners and big bands. I sang in church and high school choirs, and with the Sweet Adelines who sang barbershop quartet music. I took piano lessons and played the flute; I grooved on bluegrass and Janis Joplin in the late '60s and '70s. When I took up opera in the '80s, I was into a life-long learning curve that I still persist in following. Jer has had an equally varied life as pursuer and spectator of music.

The point here is that we have always loved music. So whatever has happened this year to our musical enjoyment, it isn't because we are more sophisticated.

No, our current pleasure comes from the specific ways we can settle into listening. We no longer sandwich music into the driven lives of making the rent, cleaning the fridge, getting home for the babysitter, and keeping up with family and friends. Nor do we feel that we have to learn and understand and figure out the musical tropes.

What we have come to, because of our age, is much better. We go to concerts as a whole event. We revel in our approaches to the concert halls—the bridge over the ravine at Reed College, the big linear park at the cultural center of Portland. We goggle at the audience and chat with other grayhairs sitting near us. We listen to the music but no longer vocalize silently or watch the violinist's fingering, wondering if we can learn to play.

We enjoy the music, and we daydream and check out the trio's interactions. We think desultory thoughts about food and the curtains that line the stage while appreciating the intertwined lines of sound. We watch the cellist look yearningly at the violist, and the violinist stretch his body as he reaches for the highest, most plaintive notes—and then it's done, and we smile and go out to dinner.

It's much simpler—and much more fun than when we were writing editorials, worrying about managerial decisions, wondering how we'd get the papers graded on time. We still have many things to attend to, but mostly they don't interfere with the occasion itself—the whole occasion, with all its pleasures. We can sit and let the event surround us.

It's the best season yet because we can take in whatever we wish, however we wish, without trying to extend it into something beyond itself.

Mama

August 12, 2019
The Fear of...

Dear Jan,

In *Still Here,* Ram Dass says that after his stroke, it wasn't the pain that was the worst; it was *the fear of pain.* Not what he felt at the moment but what he imagined he might feel later, if things got worse.

In meditation, "the fear of..." as Ram Dass describes it, is "just a thought."

Jer points out that "fear" isn't thought, and he's correct. But fear can arise from thoughts, thoughts that don't reflect the moment's reality but rather imaginary scenarios of what-ifs. Fear is useful when making plans or fleeing the danger. But it isn't helpful when the emotion has no outlet in plans or actions. In those moments "the fear of..." is "just a thought," one to be acknowledged—and with luck and practice, let go.

I realized this, again, on our trip downtown yesterday. Jer and I bussed to the center city, watched *War and Peace,* ate lunch with friends, and then trudged back to the bus stop to go home.

As I have aged, I have come to have trouble with the noise and hustle of the city. I feel pushed at from all sides, bombarded with visual stimuli—traffic and advertising lights, people walking fast, slow, with skateboards and shopping bags, cars starting, stopping, roaring engines, tooting horns, cracks in the sidewalk, transients camped out in doorways, and far too many reflective storefronts.

I remember how I once loved the city. It excited me. I wanted to be part of it. I wanted to be one of those hustling to work, to play, to sing, to dance, to drink. But now I just want to go home.

I have become dependent on Jer to guide me, to check the traffic, and to get me across streets safely. But what if Jer isn't around to keep me physically stable? What then? What will I do then?

What if I can't cope? What if I can't garden, can't shop for groceries, can't—god help me—care for him when he needs me? What if? What if? What if?

And then I remember Ram Dass's mantra, that the worst is "the fear of" pain—or the fear of confusion and inadequacy. And I remember meditation guru Andy, who reminds us that thoughts are just thoughts.

Pay attention, Andy murmurs, sit with the disorder, feel it, then let it go, and focus on the now.

And so, rather than fight with the what-if-I-can't-cope panic, I am doing what I see can be done now, writing through the chaos.

The moment—that's all there is. That's all the reality that there is.

Your Mama

The inability to deal with ordinary city life has not gotten easier, and it's probably one cause of the stereotype of the dithering old lady. But there are always the stories to intervene. In Nevada, we once rode to Death Valley with a friend who drove 25 mph, down long empty stretches of highway, never faster.

He said, when an irate driver passed him, horn blaring: "He shoulda started sooner."

And so, when we are faced with physical spaces that feel chaotic, and we notice an impatient thirty-some-year-old shouldering us out of the way, we murmur to each other: "He should have started sooner."

We laugh. It works. Whatever truths of old men and women these moments hold, they also hold personal histories. These stand us in good stead.

August 26, 2019
Suspended

Dear Jan,

The dishwasher repair guy came this morning, right on time at 9 AM. We are, now, particularly sensitive to waiting. We are waiting for surgery, scheduled for November, waiting for aftermaths, for whatever the future decides to whap us with. Waiting for repair guys is just more of the same. But the dishwasher needed repaired, and so we scheduled and expected to wait. But here he was, on time, and there he went,

19 minutes later, and now we have our whole day returned to us.

Jer and I rail against waiting: how tedious to charge off to the doctor's appointment, only to find oneself beached in the waiting room of coughing children. How tiresome to be dressed with coats on, ready to drive to friends' houses for dinner—15 minutes too early; if we go now, the host will be in the shower. We remember other lives when we were crazy busy and kept people waiting. We ran out the door, coats a-flap, apologizing as we entered the host's living room. But now, we wait at home so we won't be early, and we arrive, slightly apologetic, just a few moments before the appointed time.

Arriving at a concert early, though, can be full of pleasures—sounds of the French horns warming up, eavesdropping on the people behind you who are discussing the shoes of the house manager, checking out what different groups of people wear. It's good fun, and the waiting is part of the experience.

If I'm watering—something that I can do before the repair guy shows up—I can daydream, imagine designing large boxwood-edged gardens filled with exotic plants—plants that will be pruned by a host of elderly male gardeners who call me "ma'am." I can imagine suggesting this plant or that should be moved over there or maybe there, between the peonies—which also need to be moved. Someday I'll have to do that.

Waiting around is good, too, for clearing detritus—left-over newspapers and catalogues and dishes from last night's snacks. Thumbing idly through the Sunday *Times* satisfies my need to say I've read it. Staring at a cashmere sweater that only costs one's monthly pension is almost as good as buying it.

These are strategies to spend unfilled time, but also to keep the useless worries at bay. They provide pleasure while holding back the dam of what-ifs.

And then the repair guy shows up, finishes the job, and real actions, making lists perhaps, can begin.

Yer Mama,

Jou

September 25, 2019

The Old Trickster

Dear Jan,

You mentioned yesterday that you had been teaching Spanish at Portland Community College for exactly half your life, 27.5 years. How young we all were when we moved to Portland in 1989. You were finishing up a master's degree from the University of Kansas; Jer and I were in our mid-40s. And now we are in our late 70s and you've been a professional for all those years. Impossible. How strange, the way time can trick our brains. I am, simultaneously, age 45 and yet have always been 78 years old.

Other tricks that time plays: I'm doing various physical therapy exercises and have to time them—calf exercises are held for one minute and eye exercises for five seconds; these latter are done five times. I keep checking my instructions to remember, is this five times in one minute or one time in five minutes or something else entirely?

The devices that measure time for us are tricky. The battery-operated clock in the library, where I do my exercises, is small and tucked away, unnoticeable unless you are trying to stretch your calves for one minute. Then, its tick-tock, regular and accurate, marks every second.

In the living room the clock over the mantel, which sounds every quarter hour and bongs the hour, has time that's never quite reliable. It eyeballs its work, ball-parks seconds and minutes.

The mantle clock moves at its own pace, depending on when it was last wound, how humid it is, whether we've used the fireplace recently, and for other, quite mysterious reasons. We see that newly wound, it gallops. Then, as the days go along, it winds down. It bongs more slowly; 12 o'clock becomes an agonizing stretch. Its tick extends a long way to reach its tock.

The mantle clock is a trickster: It's not a single thing, not a single place, not even a single motion. It's a fool's journey, a contradiction to the saying "time passes so quickly when you are old."

Much of my memorable time comes in bits and pieces, an irregular lacework. Time is a line, thickening and thinning, lost to toothbrushing and dishwashing and even, sometimes, lovemaking, and then thickening with visits to a distant southern state or watching a flight of crows—or getting a medical lab report on the computer. Time, that old trickster, passes in elderhood, just as it always has, with little rhyme or reason.

Mama

October 1, 2019
Indolence

Dear Jan,

You must start your day with purpose—Prince Edward the cat demands your attention, Rick is ready with news and a plan for the day, needy students tug at your emails while you brush your teeth. But I too wake with a certain focus. I have to greet Jer, count out the pills, check my text messages, open my digital tablet, check my email, see what horrors the world perpetrated overnight, and come to the studio in readiness for writing.

Most of my activities, of course, are optional. Only the pills are essential. I could sit, hands around my coffee cup, looking blankly at the world.

But I don't.

Louise Aronson, in *Elderhood,* quotes Sharon Kaufman, a medical anthropologist who says, "The old Americans I studied do not perceive meaning in aging itself; rather, they perceive meaning in being themselves in old age."

I have always cherished those seldom-encountered mornings when I could get up and do nothing for a while. Be nothing, do nothing, feel nothing but the warm coffee cup on my hands, its liquid sliding down my throat.

But the reason I cherished—and still cherish—those kinds of mornings is because they are rare. It's their difference that makes me love them. While drinking my first cup of coffee, I tidy up my emails. I eat a healthy breakfast, just as I have been told I need to do. I read the news about events over which I have no control, just to make sure I will be the informed citizen every American has as her duty. I dutifully come to the studio to write today's note, rehearsing the last 24 hours, shaping the amorphous events.

Why do I do this? Not because I always have and not because it feels right. No, it's because part of being myself is knowing what's happening in the outside world. Part of being myself is making order out of my personal space. And part of being myself is doing something that's creative, with all of creativity's forms and meanings. Doing something beyond my own self, but attached to myself. Going to the studio and writing or inking or painting or reading poetry for the book club meeting. Making something.

Meaning comes from being myself in old age.

Mama

December 26, 2019
Flow

Dear Jan,

I just got off the phone with you—you in frozen Alaska, with plans for the evening, me in chilly Portland, feeling arthritis prickling in my thumb joints, reminding me that I am old.

Luckily you know nothing of my sorry thumbs. Knowing would interfere with your fun. Right now, I imagine you to be bundling up for your ice-skating adventure. You have told us funny stories about learning to skate at the local mall a couple of years ago. You were fifty-five and the class was otherwise composed of eight-year-olds who skated backwards by the "old lady" sitting, skates akimbo, on the ice. One little boy leaned over to ask you why you were learning to skate. And your answer was "Because I want to."

I would like to learn to skate too, but falls at my age, even skittering ones on ice, are frowned upon. They cause the med people to counsel me, once again, on Home Safety. This counsel, which always features throw rugs, starts when you approach retirement age and, after 10 or so years, wears thin. Just the thought of my doctor's horror if I mentioned ice skating makes me grin.

But I like to watch, from Monti's, the 20-year-old running for the bus, shouting cheerily as she gains on the open door. It's fun to see the middle schoolers on their bicycles, coming down the sidewalk in front of our house, circling and dipping and rearing, pumping faster and faster until one ducks down a driveway to the street, and the rest follow in a flood, off to find another sidewalk to perform on.

Sometimes the body messes up and the eight-year-old flops on the ice or the bicyclist turns too quickly, but the bodies look graceful and fluid, even in their flailing.

And then I get to wondering about my own unfluid jerkiness—how can I make it a gain rather than a loss?

Well, here are some things I have done.

Knowing that I often drop things led me to find better designed glasses. Putting the heavy hot water pot on a low counter was a triumph. Not filling everything to the brim (where it's bound to dump itself on your new blouse), ah, very helpful. There's a pleasure in adjusting my world according to my needs, not those that young designers thought up years ago.

I take a weird delight in working through problems—ah, yes, I can't raise my arm that high any more. Well, other arm? Let Jerry do it? Move the object to a lower shelf? Which shall it be?

No use in going to the gym to strengthen the rotator cuff—it's as healthy as it's ever going to be. Deciding whether a rug for your cold feet is worth more than sending it to Goodwill as Safe Home advises involves thoughtful evaluation of the coldness of the room, the kind of rug available, the question of a new rug—or new floor finish.

Maintaining my body entitles me to extra pleasures (like a mimosa at Monti's). And I can discard a despised chore like using that upper shelf for my favorite glasses. Phooey on that.

There's another joy—*phooey on that*! What a grand phrase!

I can take a serious pleasure in our slow quotidian walks through the neighborhood, being that nosy old lady who chats with children and adults alike, who worries about neighbors who are sick or injured, and who notes whether the newbies in the house down the street are friendly or uppish. I love seeing houses getting fixed—new roofs and better siding and new sewer pipes. These are pleasures that differ from physical fluidity and are good for the slow, observant walker.

Water ripples over rocks as well as pushing around them.

Mama

January 26, 2021
Desultory

Dear Jan,

Aside from—or sharply contrasting to—parsing out the intellectual puzzles of Great Books, I find myself spending time ensconced in wooliness, muffled and cozy. I stare at bare tree branches. I note a chickadee bouncing off twigs in the maple. I spot a black-headed Harris's sparrow on the deck, looking for seeds. I see shrubs that are sprouting new stems. I contemplate pruning. I write absent-mindedly about what I see. It's like coming back from a surgery, wrapped in anesthesia.

The forsythia has its buds but it's not yet time to harvest branches to bring inside. Yesterday I pruned our rosa rugosa to within six inches of the soil, hoping to discourage it from savaging the beauty bushes next to it.

The rugosa has its revenge: I have a thorn embedded in the crease between my left palm and index finger. The burning redness reminds me I was not thinking good thoughts as I snipped and removed gangly, dangerous branches. Nature has its little ways.

Desultory writing is a hoot. I never know what I might find as I bounce around in my idle thoughts—today, while observing an errant squirrel, I remembered stories derived from the Greek *Odyssey,* stories found, for example, in Tennyson's poem, which, like James Joyce's novel, is called "Ulysses."

Tennyson writes of the warrior-wanderer, Ulysses, who "cannot rest from travel" and "will drink Life to the lees." In the poem Ulysses sees Telemachus, his son (who is the model for Joyce's Dedalus) as a prudent and boring bureaucrat:

> This is my son, mine own Telemachus,
> To whom I leave the scepter and the isle,
> ...
> This labor, by slow prudence to make mild
> A rugged people, and through soft degrees
> Subdue them to the useful and the good.
> Most blameless is he, centered in the sphere
> Of common duties, decent not to fail
> In offices of tenderness, and pay
> Meet adoration to my household gods
> When I am gone. He works his work, I mine.

Tennyson, wishing to drink life to the lees, does not admire the good functionary Telemachus. It is unclear whether Joyce admires his Dedalus. I am detached from both of them, wrapped in bemused disengagement.

And so it goes, a slow morning pricked by a rose thorn, now drifting into a lazy afternoon. Did Telemachus have moments when he found prudent thinking to be tiresome? What if we changed the genders of these characters—would the prudent female Telemachus have had an affair while her father was gallivanting and wenching about the Mediterranean? Would she have shouted rude obscenities at the squirrels, frantically digging up her tulip bulbs? Would she have ripped out the wretched rugosa, using a chain saw?

And so my random thoughts go—nowhere.

June

III

HIS & HERS: HELLO CANCER

Getting older is not a stroll but an ambush. —Andrew Solomon

Aug 2, 2019
Turn, Turn, Turn

Dear Jan,

Today I find myself turned upside down by new happenings. I have to adjust.

Jer has prostate cancer. He had biopsies on Wednesday, came home with bleeding, and almost passed out in the shower. He has no lasting repercussions from his blood loss, but he has seen the lab reports. They show cancer. He is to consult with his urologist next week to decide what comes next.

This is not a notice of the end. Cancer can be tended to, with pain inevitable but more life, too, perhaps good life. It wasn't the probability of his death that woke me at midnight, and 2 AM and 4. It was that Jer won't allow me to be with him when he gets the official notification during the consult with his doctor.

I need to know what's happening. I don't understand why, after 56 years together, I won't be part of this discussion. I am shattered by his decision.

He doesn't want me with him. He says that I won't be able to keep quiet, that having me there will change the dynamic, that I will ask uncalled-for questions. I could not reassure him. Saying that I will respect his primacy didn't stop his stubborn reserve. Insisting that I need to know because we are a unit had no effect.

I keep reiterating my arguments. I say I should be there to take notes. I could read the doctor's body language. We could talk about what each of us heard. I said all this to him, but he remained obdurate.

This afternoon you, Jan, and Sam, who is visiting in Portland, will show up, and we will not mention Jer's medical status. We will discuss your upcoming trip to Isle Royale in Michigan, and you, suddenly realizing that no one has asked about us, will bring up the gardens. I will discuss the salvia and sunflowers, the watering chores and which plants died because of the summer drought.

And now, having written about your kinwork, your careful inclusion of everyone in our conversations, I feel my resentment start to fade. Each person needs to be acknowledged in personal ways, ways which allow for changes that time, status, and yes, age, bring.

Elderhood is a different place in my relationship with Jer; I must develop a tolerance for his new needs as well as tending to my own. He hasn't faced many medical crises in our lives together; this is how he needs to deal with them. And I will find a way to deal with my own feelings of desertion. And figure out how to soften the twist in my stomach when I think about all this.

I love you.

Mama

It took a couple of weeks, until late August, for Jer and me to talk again about his rejection of my presence during that first cancer consult. His explanation was simpler than any I had thought of.

Jer feared he would not be able to control himself when officially presented with the news of his cancer. If I were present, my sympathy would make him more vulnerable to breakdown. He wanted to face, without flinching, what he feared most.

I remember when Brown Cat had to be euthanized; Jer did not want me to go with him to the vet for those last moments. For the same reason. If I were present, he said, he feared he could not face the cat's death with strength and dignity.

So, the unhappiness I felt about being rejected was in fact false. It wasn't about me. A good lesson but a hard one to learn. It's not always about me.

August 8, 2019
Into a New Phase

Dear Jan,

Yesterday Jer was officially told by an oncologist that his prostate cancer is "aggressive" and will require surgery. A nasty word, "aggressive." More tests are scheduled, but these are mostly for deciding where to cut.

I am bewildered. I don't know how to think about this. Should I be frightened? Agonized? Succumbing to an inchoate pain? Should I put the confusion aside to make preparations, and if so, preparations for what? We did our "watchful waiting" earlier this summer. Now the time is upon us.

We aren't prepared for this, although it is exactly what millions have faced, and we had been given a lot of advance warnings—so why are we confused? Why is it so bewildering? And why can't I get my mouth (meaning my mind, my brain, my emotions) around this changed state of our lives.

Because, of course, it is *our* lives we are talking about here. Not other people's, but ours. Mine. My life. His life. And it's going to be a new phase of our lives, times we have not lived through before. I don't know how to *be* in this new set of circumstances.

We will muddle along.

And so, I am announcing that we have apparently arrived at a new stage of development. And in the same announcement, I say that we haven't given up any of the other pieces of our lives—the gardening, art making, the cooking, the walking, the talking. We will deal with it because we have no choice. We will do the best we can at the moments that arrive. That is all.

We will muddle along, with each other. That is all.

Mama

A lot of fine writers have described and explored these moments of recognition—knowledge of one's helplessness and the emotions that such knowledge brings forth. But at this moment, for me—and I'm guessing, for Jer—the emotions were chaotic and incoherent. All we could think of to do was plan and continue our days, blanking out the fears as best we could because we had to go on.

August 13, 2019
The Same River

Hi hi, my luv,

This morning seems more manageable.

Jer is cheerful, I watered a bit, moved a hose around, dead-headed some brown blooms, made tea, listened to music, poured some vermillion ink onto Japanese paper, and now I'm in front of the computer, talking to you. The sun shines and the keyboard responds. This moment is good.

Some days it is easier to open ourselves to pain, or to the fear of pain, than to contentment, even to joy. But this morning, I find myself opening to pleasure. Much better.

Mama

During hard times, daily activities became more important. I still faithfully brushed my teeth after the announcement, and I fed the hydrangeas while thinking about cancer and prostate surgery. I laid out my art papers and poured ink on them. I shaped and hung brass and golden and silver wires, climbing the ladder to dangle them from rafters to floor. I moved them, thin and wispy, so the sun hit them from different directions.

The wires, swaying in tiny breezes, became shape-shifters as they twisted in the light. Life kept moving while I gardened and mourned and resented. The quotidian, in all its variety, kept on going.

August 25, 2019
And So, On It Goes

Dear Jan,

I am making lists. Lists to survive.

We (Jer and I) have read and discussed the MRI report, the pathologist report, and the oncologist's diagnosis: aggressive prostate cancer.

We (Jer and I) have discussed, bawled, laid awake, gone into deep sleeps, spent relentless nights, watered our coffee with tears, discussed our feelings (lightly), gotten angry and despairing, had bruising disagreements, lost and then found on the side cabinet some necessary paperwork. We have teared up, cried, laid awake, and slept too deeply.

I finally told you the news of Jer's cancer on Friday, while he was having a full body scan at the hospital. Sitting on the couch, we (you and I) had a meltdown in each other's arms and then sat back up, holding hands.

We (you and I) proceeded to cry, laugh, laugh (and cry) at ourselves laughing. We told each other that we knew all along that something was wrong, that he didn't look good; I described Jer's reactions, you offered advice from your own cancer experiences. I wrote down ideas for research; we told stories of other hard times. We disagreed about whether to tell grandson Sam, because you thought he would be hurt if he were blind-sided after the fact, while I thought not burdening him too early might be helpful. We went with your instinct, of course.

Jer and I spoke of his refusal to allow me to go with him for that first consult. He was sure he would not be able to control his emotions. His desire was to face what he had to face. So, it was not about me.

We now know that surgery will take place in a couple of months. We'll have time to prepare. We'll have time to wait. We'll have time to organize our thoughts.

And last night Prince Edward the cat escaped the house and bloodied you when you grabbed him from under the rhododendron bush.

Jeezus. What a week.

Mama

I have been told that this list of our week is too tidy, too controlled. Making the list ignores the messiness and humanity of the crisis. I agree. But (and you knew there would be a "but") when the world is out-of-control, making lists feels essential. Of course my stomach hurt, my bowels tightened, my head exploded. Of course I walked and walked and walked, faster and faster, trying to escape my own thoughts. But throughout the walks I also made lists—lists of what had to be done before the surgery. What groceries and dry goods needed to be bought. Who would I call for which medical emergencies? What insurance referrals were needed? What bank accounts checked? What did I have to do to stay sane? What did I have to do to keep Jer sane? What should I do for you, Jan, to keep you sane? Sam wrote notes, of course, and tried to say comforting things. I was grateful, but inarticulate.

In a NY Times Magazine *article (July 10, 2022) Virginia Eubanks writes about the aftermath of a traumatic beating her husband endured, a mugging which damaged him physically and emotionally for years afterward. She says, "Fighting through the aftermath of the attack was exhausting, But it was also very simple, all action and no feeling."*

Our experience was nothing as horrific as Ms. Eubanks', but "all action and no feeling" comes close to describing the path I felt I had to take. It's a strategy that can work, a strategy that I have used many times in my life. It got me through this event too.

In the back of my mind, of course, rolled and still rolls the question of whether I will be able to manage this kind of list-and-action strategy when I'm 81 or 85 or 90. But we got through, this time.

August 27, 2019
Suspended, Yet Again

Dear Jan,

Everyone spends a lot of time waiting, but standing around, restless, seems most prevalent in adolescence—and in elderhood. Adolescents are waiting to grow up or to have a driver's license or their first sex. Elders wait around in a doctor's office, for the handyman to fix the sink, for the next round of chemo. We wait for the days of testing, the diagnosis, the surgery. We wait, as the wiseacres in nursing homes say, "for the Big Scythe."

The trick, I'm hoping, is to know that waiting around is part of our necessary existence. It's not a plot against us. It's not something outrageous. It is what it is. Age means waiting.

Andy, the meditation guru, would probably advise facing the "waiting," acknowledging it, and letting it go. But what about the pain behind the waiting, the days when I can't see the finches or imagine a grand garden? What about standing around waiting, not for the first guest or the dishwasher repairman, but for information about the rest of our lives?

OK, an admission: we are waiting for the appointment with the oncologist with further test results from Jer's bone scan and lymph node MRI. We are waiting to hear just how bad his cancer is.

Ram Dass says the fear of pain is worse, perhaps, than the pain itself. I'm acknowledging this.

Tears are leaking from my eyes and down the side of my nose. I'm acknowledging the wet.

And then, having written all that, I find myself smiling wryly at the rhetoric, at the use of language, to encapsulate this waiting day.

These are just thoughts. No pain has yet been inflicted or occurred. Only the fear of.

And so, today, I will write this note, deadhead the pink rose, read *The NY Times* "1619" series, walk to Monti's, water the hydrangea, parboil and freeze the peaches, do my email, and help with dinner.

That should get us to bedtime. Then there's meditation and waiting for morning.

When I think this way, I find both pain and comfort. The pain is in the pointlessness of the activities I've mentioned above. And the pleasure, as I've already pointed out, is also in the activities, however pointless they are.

What's the Yeats' line? "An aged man is but a paltry thing / A tattered coat upon a stick..."

Yeats lived a long time, wrote over many years, and says a lot about aging. He never gives up—an aged man may be a paltry thing—"unless / Soul clap its hand and sing." He writes, "Bodily decrepitude is wisdom," and, "Accomplished fingers begin to play. / Their eyes mid many wrinkles, their eyes, / Their ancient, glittering eyes, are gay."

"Cast a cold eye/ On life, on death. / Horseman, pass by." That's Yeats.

And so, along with Andy and Ram Dass, I add Yeats. "Cast a cold eye," says Yeats. "Read some poetry," says Underwood.

If nothing else, the parsing out and thinking about the words and rhymes and sound of language will pass the time. Tomorrow, the cold eye. Today, horseman, pass by.

June

These late summer / early autumn days rolled on and Jer and I waited. We lived our lives, thought our thoughts, I recorded dailinesses that appear elsewhere in this book. The surgery was scheduled for November. We moved through tests and biopsies, consultations, and appointments. We also gardened, ate, walked, and lived. Most of those mundane times—appointments and walks—started to sound too much alike. My daily renditions became tiresome.

The days between August 27 and November 4, 2019 were mundane, consisting of the slowest of quotidians, ordinary and banal. Underneath those days was the thrum of low-level anxiety. The anxiety was an off-key base, occasionally rising to a screeching 10 or so bars , but mostly just subterranean chords, accompanying my gardening, the cat-talking, our friendly greetings. We moved through those times, that noiseless noise. Boring and terrifying.

October 6, 2019
And So It Goes

Dear Jan,

The discussed parts of aging are the physical changes, the winding down of energy, the ailments, the losses, the pains, and the suffering.

We elders complain. You adults worry. And I imagine people asking you with wringing hands: "How are the Aged P's doing, health-wise?"

And now, here we are, facing Jer's surgery for prostate cancer. Talking about this new situation turns out to be surprisingly difficult. It's confusing to our shared language and long-standing communication styles. He dislikes discussing physical ailments. He carries his worries to end scenarios, without much of anything in-between. I do the logistics: first we'll do this and then, if that doesn't work, we'll move to option B.

We talk past one another.

We find ourselves moving in halting manner through various parts of the conversation—I detail the next steps, the buying of paper towels and the cooking of casseroles; Jer works out what I need to know about handling the bills after he dies; where I will find his computer passwords; where pension and Social Security checks are deposited. But these strategies avoid speaking of what we are feeling. When I thought he was in physical pain, he was actually grieving. When I thought I detected anxiety, he was doing income calculations.

We seem to lack any language to get to those feelings. Perhaps we lack insight into what the other is going through.

After all these years of marriage, I thought I knew how to read Jer's reticence; I knew when he was angry or depressed or absorbed in thought or hungry. I knew what strategies and tactics were best suited to his emotional states. He was pretty good at reading my moods, too. But the upcoming surgery requires a different language, perhaps emotions that we have not managed to bring to the surface. Certainly, we need new strategies.

Uncharted ways to navigate—so basic that at first we didn't notice how confused we could be. I'm sure we will learn to communicate fully again, just as we learned to do so over all the other 56 years. But in the moment, the comfort recedes before the panic of the unreadable, the blankness with which Jer looks at me when I try to allay his fears.

I love you, my ducks,
Mama

I have been asked if I had advice for those going through these kinds of states, particularly as they reach that new stage of human development, elderhood.

I'm not one for giving advice. For me, the best writing serves up human experience rather than drawing aphorisms about it. I'm a reader of novels, and I believe that seeing the struggle, the exhaustion, the sorrows, and the joys of others on the written page has helped me lead my own life.

But the novels I love are not necessarily those that Jer likes or that you, Jan, exclaim over. We are individuals with different needs and different takes, on different days. It's why Jer and I mistook each other's moods and desires when our lives were so altered. It's why I'm writing—not because I know what it all means or can give anyone advice about life; it's because something here may provide a reader with an insight, a way to go on, a vision of how the struggle felt to me, and what came out of that struggle: "We can't go on. We will go on."

And since October 2019, Jer and I have re-formed our ways of communicating. We discuss aches and pains and feelings more freely. We not only tell each other of our love, but we also ask each other about hangnails, eye-strain, painful knees and sleep patterns. A big change, in our middling elderhood.

October 21, 2019
The Music Marches On

Dear Jan,

I'm sitting in the studio with the All Classical station playing one of those pieces that features lots of squalling violins and pounding drums, moving us toward its inevitable conclusion. Others may imagine it goes toward its great triumph—Boom, boom, boom… *alla Marcia.* I'm finding it merely strident, relentless in its marchings.

This is Beethoven, the *Consecration of the* House *Overture, Opus 124.* Today I have no use for consecrating marches.

Our morning was driven by preparations for the surgery. Jer has been laying in supplies for me—as you joked last week, he will have enough canned beans and toilet paper stashed in the basement to survive a category nine earthquake. Because I don't drive and will be taking buses to shop, it is good to stock up on heavy and bulky staples.

Yesterday we took care of other neglected items; we got my old Tivoli CD player working again. And we updated our TV so the broadcast stations from our antenna would work. This morning's trials were a bit less successful. I need to find an endodontist who doesn't dismiss my concerns about a bad tooth, and Jer needs some button-down-the-front pajama shirts for the surgery. When did all male PJs become over-the-head outfits, anyway?

And so it goes, boring and frustrating, and necessary, until the day comes when it won't matter what hasn't been done.

The music will change, and the relentless march will become a *largo*.

At the end of our morning's frustrations, we went to Monti's where I had the consoling breakfast of berries, yogurt, and cottage cheese, and Jer rummaged through a pleasant memory of Parkrose Hardware. Maybe that's not the *largo*, but rather the sprightly *allegretto*. I would try for *largamente*, but that's not my style— "dignified style" happens only when I'm really pissed off, and today I missed that mode altogether.

And so, not Beethoven, perhaps, just jou, in preparation for this next sequence, *misterioso*.

And I highly recommend *Wikipedia*'s article on Italian musical terms—it made me smile.

Your Ma

October 22, 2019
Cookery

Dear Jan,

Jer, who usually writes with me and keeps me accountable, is off grocery shopping today. Again. He had a long list of food and sundries to buy and was only slightly dismayed when I added more.

I have my own agenda, of course; awaiting my attention is the cooking and freezing of dinners for the surgery and recovery.

Although cooking is thought of as a womanly skill and I have sometimes imagined myself to be womanly, cooking is not one of my skills. I cooked for family for years—and some years I did better than others. We exchanged vegetarian meals with our Kansas buddies, Bruce and Jane, and I cooked those. I had some triumphs with the pureed meals I made for you during your cancer healing, and the Sunday breakfast gatherings when Sam was at Reed College. These were specialized skills, highly dependent upon doing the same thing over and over again. I'm very good at coconut custard and buckwheat pancakes.

But knowing that Jer, who has been the prime cook for the last few years, will be laid up, today I took a deep breath and found a recipe. We will have white bean soup for dinner and freeze the remainder.

In my mind, I label this activity in all caps: TODAY I COOK.

This will be a constant in my brain. Before his surgery, Jer and I will go for coffee at Monti's, we will walk and count steps, and we will spend hours in front of computers. And I will COOK.

Sigh.

I love to eat. Other people's cooking is delightful. I love the conversations where we share meals with good friends. But when I sit down at a meal that I've cooked, I barely taste it. Exhaustion, sometimes mixed with the tales of friends and laughter, makes me oblivious to the food itself. After the stories have been told and glasses refilled and the guests departed, I need a potato chip.

However, I'm off to the kitchen. At 77, it may be time for me to lean into my womanliness.

June

October 29, 2019
Quotidians of a Sort

Dear Jan,

Jer is raking leaves after a steady (I want to say "studied") wind that flowed all night. The wind had swept the back drive, but made tidy rows and piles on the deck. It had laid maple leaves thick onto the front porch and inundated the front driveway. It had blown in just at the moment the branches were ready to let go of their golden camouflage.

I am waiting for the rat catcher. His name is Chance, but my Victorian novel reading makes me think of him as The Rat Catcher. We have rats in the attic. They make a racket in the walls just as the sun goes down, and it feels like they might chew their way through the ceiling. They are raising families there. So, the traps were set and two have been caught. More are scrambling around. The Rat Catcher will make his way through the attic insulation, pick up the dead bodies and lay out more poison.

We are also waiting for November 4, the day of Jer's surgery. Five days. Five days to get through. I have put off the root canal until he recovers, and my physical therapy for the vestibular problem has been put on indefinite hold.

The unhappiness, uneasiness, and anxiety come and go in waves. Some days we are grateful for the calm lives we lead and the gorgeous fall that surrounds us. Other days fill with dread. I suspect it will feel easier when the day of the surgery comes, at least for a short, logistical-filled bit. And then we'll see. Sometimes I yearn for that clean sweep like the wind, arranging everything in tidy windrows.

In the meantime, the sound of the rake against the sidewalk outside continues, the washer cleans the clothes, the tea is warm and comforting, and I'm keeping my head in a neutral position, as suggested by the vestibular therapist. And I love you,
Ma

This note, dated October 29, was the last until November 24. It was a blank time, a time of doing what came next, with no markers, no ways to capture and shape the mists.

Medical events, for me, are simply to be lived through.

November 24, 2019
Start Up

Dear Jan,

So here I am again, almost a month after Jer's surgery, his after-surgery complications, after my panics and recoveries from panics, his stabilization and slow return to movement and energy. Now, a kind of stasis.

Two thoughts about living through this month: the first is that my mantra *I can do this* got me through a lot of bad moments. And the second—*This recovery, this time*—has been a constant refrain, the recognition that nothing stays the same. Decay is as inevitable as growth. Change is our only constant.

"I can do this"—I repeated again and again when "aggressive cancer" popped up unwanted in my mind. Before Jer's surgery, I walked alone in Portland's twilight, repeating to myself, "I can do this." I said it silently in the surgery waiting room, and then afterward, beside him in the recovery room. I said it while taking him warm tea during those first post-op days, when he sat in his armchair, white-faced. I repeated it again during the ambulance ride after he passed out at 3 AM. I said to you, Jan, when you took me off for coffee later that morning and I had the meltdown of exhaustion, sitting in a hospital alcove, sobbing; after you fed me a breakfast burrito and brought me hot coffee, I wiped my tears and said, aloud, "I can do this."

The most insistent moment of "I can do this" was when I tripped and landed on my face, hurrying to catch a ride to the hospital. A few days post-surgery, Jer's gut had seized up, and then, after he lost consciousness in the middle of the night, he went back into the hospital, where they waited for his intestines to start moving again. It took a while. That morning, when I was rushing to meet Susan, my foot caught on the edge of the deck and I sprawled, face down in the gravel next to a concrete stepping stone.

When I felt the blood trickling down my forehead, I laid in the gravel and wondered what and how badly I had damaged myself. I moved various parts. I sat up on a skinned elbow. I said, as loud and fierce as I could manage: "OK, June. You can do this."

And then, I stumbled to Susan's house, she wiped off the blood, peroxided my forehead, declared the injuries minimal, John rescued my bags, and we drove to the hospital, where I chatted Jer up until you came and took me off the lounge and allowed me to collapse in a bout of sniveling. You brought me coffee until I pulled myself together saying, "I can do this." In a different tone of voice, because I could, at that time, in that place, with the help of friends and family, do it.

And now we are home, things are pretty well fixed for the nonce, our routines re-established, the house back in shape, Jer adjusting and still not complaining, our wry laughter rising, his wit and my delight in it intact. We made it.

This time. Because it's life. Health is temporary, competence won't always be available, and there will be a time when I can't do it. But for now, I did it—he did it—we did it—this time.

That's really all there is. Done, like the end of the marathon or a semester's work with an especially difficult student. Done, and we all did it. Until next time.

Your ma
Who thanks you

Two years later we can say with assurance that Jer's surgery was successful. No cancer at the margins. The surgeon reports that he "got it all." The bad after-effects were disconcerting, long months of Jer struggling to get through post-op anemia, feeling like he might be starting the long slide to the end. But finally we came to a level place, and his recovery, with few setbacks, settled into the easier groove of general aging. Stories for another day.

November 27, 2019
The Day Before Thanksgiving

Dear Jan,

Jer and I were sitting in front of the fire the other night, a chilly night after a gray day, him in his pajamas, covered with the cozy throw, me lying on the couch. We looked at each other and smiled.

We were content. Our books, our companionship, the warmth of the fire, the soft knowledge that this time we made it through—content.

And I thought of my trip to Monti's Café earlier that day.

I needed to get some lunch food. I wanted to regain, after my long Jer-surgery lay-off, my normal walking route, and so I took the long way to Monti's. Chili, I thought: Monti's chili is bland but full of good stuff. Going there will push me to make the longer walk I've been avoiding.

So I set off, past our friend's houses—the Salings, who supported me through the hospital days, the Graves, who delivered salmon dinner last Saturday, on past Shelly's, who waves to us through her windows.

But I wasn't thinking of those people as I walked, even as I passed a crew of workers doing something to Arlene's chimney. Mostly I thought about....

Well, what did I think about? Not how I was feeling. Not about my ever-present vertigo or the crows that were fussing at me from the wires. Not about the cats who mewed at me along the route, nor the chickens or new fencing of houses along the route. No, I worried. I fussed. I tried to make plans.

Should I get two bowls or three of Monti's chili? Would Jer's stomach be able to handle the chili beans? Will he be OK by himself until I get back? Will the car coming fast up Burnside stop for me? How far should I walk before I make the turn to Monti's? Was I going too far, leaving Jer alone too long?

I noticed nothing, not the kids—Six, Seven, and Eight—or roofing crews or crows or cats or even people.

I was totally inward, planning for contingencies, taking on what-ifs. I wrapped myself in thoughts, as if I had no eyes, mouth, ears. Someone said hello, I glanced, saw nothing, and went back to thinking. What if, when, call Jer, no, he'll be napping, what if....

Only at Monti's, where Rachel and Anastasia asked, with earnest concern, where we had been the last month, did some of the hardness soften, breaking through my obsessed worrying. I asked about their Thanksgiving plans, found that Anastasia's mother from Alaska was visiting. Rachel was going to eat with family in Washington. I chatted with a couple of women wanting to buy soup, and then sat in one of the tall stools, waiting for the take-out bag. I took the shortest way home, feeling relieved that Jer had not had to call. And then too, I felt lighter because I had had human communication at the café, casual chatting, which brought me back to the moment.

That evening, I read a book review in *The NY Times*; in it, the reviewer says the book asks, "What is your pleasure?"

The question, the reviewer writes, "plays out across the arc of the book" and expands upon it. "Where do we find pleasure? How do we find language for it? How do we create narratives that hold the kinds of happiness that exist not in superlative moments but across long durations: "The pleasure of abiding. The pleasure of insistence, of persistence. The pleasure of obligation, the pleasure of dependency. The pleasures of ordinary devotion."

I thought of how I couldn't grasp the pleasure of the walk to Monti's, of how my imagination prevented me from breathing easily and reaching outward. Only under the kind eyes of the women who served up soup could I bring myself back to the present. And then, I walked home, gazing at crows and whispering to cats; I heated up the soup, fulfilling my "obligation" to dinner, devoting myself to Jer's comfort and in doing these ordinary things, I could feel the pleasures of abiding, persistence, obligation, and dependency. The pleasures of ordinary devotion.

Mama

January 4, 2020
A Grump

Dear Jan,

I'm in a pissy mood this morning. Just a plain old grump.

I snapped at Jer about his pacing about the house. He does it to increase his strength, but this morning it got on my nerves. Mine was not a loving response to his needs, but there you have it. I'm grumpy.

The grump is tied to the report from my "enhanced" mammogram and ultrasound tests on Thursday. That report means more tests, i.e., a needle biopsy.

I'm also faced with a root canal on Monday. Did I say I was grumpy?

I swore I wouldn't get into medical nuisances but here I am, ta-ta.

Ta-ta is a sardonic shorthand for "so goes it" uttered with an ironic shrug. "What's to do about this shit?"

Isn't the word "sardonic" a grand one: it ices the cake of grumpiness!

I am amused by how much better I feel, writing down these bitches and moans. I never liked my naval-gazing diary entries—doing them made me feel sloppy and stupid. But right now, bitching and moaning cheers me up.

After leaving Jer to his house pacing, I came to the studio to write. I looked with disdain at the art I did yesterday. I cleaned up a bunch of brushes, threw away scattered papers, and then poured and dripped and smeared over the drawing I did yesterday.

Now I feel better.

And now I can say it. At age 77 I have medical problems. This morning's grumps are about tests for breast cancer and root canals, so I feel a certain self-righteousness. Shall I recite the ills of the world, how it's blowing up, burning up, being violated? No, I shan't. My own ills are perfectly sufficient, thank you.

I hope you aren't too grumpy today, m'dear. I hope I haven't hurt Jer's feelings too much. I know for sure, this too will pass. Not that that makes my grumpiness less. Only splooging on paper, both with ink and computer pixels makes me feel better. Anything that works, works!

Mama

January 11, 2020
Gender Equity

Dear Jan,

His and hers cancers—a bit of dark humor. The marriage of equals at 77—first Jer's prostate cancer has to be removed, and then I learn my breast "mass" needs to be dug out.

My beloved gynecologist, Lydia Collins, who received the pathologist's report first, was vague about what comes next. But she called me immediately because she knew I would see the lab results online, and she wanted me to know that she was supportive. I appreciated her thoughtfulness, but was stunned by the news. I muttered thank you and hung up.

The biopsy had been painful. It shocked my system, made my legs bounce uncontrollably. The nurse assigned to watch me for just these reactions stroked my back and gave me a warm blanket and a private room to recover in. She called Jer and made sure I was OK to walk with him to the car. And today, I'm realizing that, after all these years of taking my breasts for granted, watching them with a kind of bemused detachment as they enlarged with weight gain and then fell with gravity's pull, suddenly I'm not detached or bemused at all.

You were here yesterday when the call from Dr. Collins came, and so you got the news at the same time we did. And then you stayed, and our Friday morning conversation went on, oddly normal. We skirted the subject and discussed marriage and its various conditions and negotiations. But of course, we were not thinking much about the conversation.

And then you gave us hugs and ran off, presumably to talk to Rick about cancer and breasts and prostates and to do some online research, just to know more.

And so, his and her cancers—well, I guess we can work on that. We'll navigate the unknowns—how much information is useful and how much is too much? How much pissing and moaning can one make before one becomes tiresome? How much pestering of the medical profession is useful and when does it become counter-productive?

At some point in the middle of last night, I thought, OK, this too will come about and will pass into something more. It's just life, and the little jokes about negotiating the ailments will go on. We will either establish new norms of behavior, or we'll apologize and go back to the old ones. We'll figure it out as we go along.

But then this morning, all I wanted to do was to crawl into bed with Jer and get held. But he was already in the kitchen, fully dressed, making breakfast, laying out our pills—we gave each other a hug. I reconciled myself to the upright state: a hug is good and coffee is good and the turned-up heat was good and the paper and lights and nice smells, all good. The linear narrative of the quotidian. That word, again!

Mama

And then we waited, just as we had for word about what would happen next with Jer's cancer. It turns out that that's part of the process.

January 17, 2020
So They Say

Dear Jan,

I'm trying to work through ethical and personal conundrums. Today's puzzles:

Questions. How many medical tests are too many? Should I do more research? Do I excise the suspicious mass and extend the nation's medical costs, perhaps without any personal benefit? Am I medicalizing my life rather than living it? How can one research these questions, anyway? And what is our moral duty now that we've reached middlin' old age? And how do the ethics jive with our emotions and possibilities?

These are questions that are more easily answered at age 50 or 60, when of course you take all measures to stay alive. You have a long life to enjoy and to contribute to society. But at age 78?

Just to update with details: the breast "excision" is a lumpectomy which takes out an amorphous batch of tissue, probably but not certainly cancerous, for the pathologist to examine. In the best scenario, it's just a lump of ordinary breast tissue. Second best is that it's got some cancer, but all has been removed and so radiation won't follow; radiation, and possibly chemo, would follow if the ball of flesh they cut out of my breast turns out to be cancerous and messy.

It's surgery and bound to hurt. Not as major a surgery as Jer's but maybe with more pain simply because breasts are designed to be sensitive.

And so, should I wait a couple of years and see? No, says the pathologist. No, says the oncologist surgeon. And, no, say June and Jer.

But June keeps pondering the decision. Barbara Ehrenreich is quoted by Parul Sehgal (in *The NY Times*, April 10, 2018). Sehgal writes:

At 76 years old, Ehrenreich has decided that she is old enough to die. She forswears annual exams, cancer screenings and any other measure "expected of a responsible person with health insurance. … Not only do I reject the torment of a medicalized death, but I refuse to accept a medicalized life."

It's reasonable, even honorable to so coolly make peace with the inevitable. But I [Sehgal] confess wanting a bit more raging against the dying of the light. Ehrenreich is irreplaceable to the culture, with her rigor and skepticism, her allergy to comforting illusions. … The wellness movement, as you might imagine, doesn't stand a chance. She fillets it with ease and relish …

"Ehrenreich's focus," says Sehgal, "makes it clear that [Ehrenreich's] is a book born out of private not public concerns…. It possesses what the critic Helen Vendler described as "the strange binocular style" of late works, in which the writer is attentive to death's encroaching shadow but also vividly alive to the present moment. There is a feeling of Ehrenreich getting her affairs in order, slaying a few final foes."

I decide that, at this time, notwithstanding Ehrenreich's arguments, a medical intervention is what I want. I will have the surgery. I will rage a bit longer. With the permission of the surgeon, we will spend February in Arizona. Then we will come home to face the knife.

Jer had no doubts about the prostate operation; he had done the conservative wait-and-watch thing for years prior to his third biopsy. But the oncologist in my case says the excision of the mass is essential. Watch-and-wait (except for the short reprieve in Arizona) is not advisable. But still, doubt lingers. "Procedure." "Excision." Such calm words for something I know is going to hurt like hell.

Hugs,
Mama

I was not brave about breast cancer. But I continue to be reminded that, as we are alive, life will be a wild mélange of experiences and sensations: ever it was thus. Medical adventures are just one more aspect of our daily existences. Life is multitudinous, replicating, modulating, modifying, cranking up, and pushing down and occasionally even popping up with new developments.

If this were a novel, or an account of a personal trauma, overcome or succumbed to, the thread would be singular—perhaps wildly colored, and with frayed edges, but nevertheless, like a Beethoven finale, moving toward a final chord. But real life as an elder is too muddled and has too many threads to focus on only one. There's too much of the quotidian to be recorded. And so, my thoughts about the impending surgery and its outcomes sometimes got dismissed, acknowledged, and let go of, forgotten. This is not denial; it was simply the way life went on. Goes on.

On February 1, 2020, we drove from Portland to Astoria, Oregon, and down the Pacific coast, through the California Redwoods, and on to the cactus delights of the Sonoran desert and Tucson, Arizona. Photos of that trip and our four week stay in the Tucson area can be found in our blog: https://southeastmain.wordpress.com/2020/02/14/the-annual-adventure-on-the-road/

Then, in early March 2020, the U.S. became inundated with the Covid 19 virus. It was a pandemic. We read of it on our laptops sitting in the cactus desert of Oro Valley. Hospitals were overrun, flights canceled, rumors of internal borders being closed were circulating. We needed to get home. We abandoned our rental cottage, packed the car, and said goodbye to our Tucson buddy, meeting her in the last restaurant we were to enter for the next two years. We ate on the road, maskless because we knew nothing of the airborne nature of the virus. We washed our hands obsessively and drove faster. On March 12, we were back in Portland. On the morning of the 13th Jer shopped for groceries and dry goods, and we, vulnerable elders, self-isolated.

Some entries from our return to Portland with photos of our outdoor pandemic retreat space (the Pad) can also be found on the blog: https://southeastmain.wordpress.com/2020/05/27/the-pad-or-how-i-am-spending-my-pandemic/

Monday March 16, 2020
Back Home, in the Midst of Covid-19

Dear Jan,

Home in the middle of the first Covid crisis has involved a flurry of text messaging. Kinwork via cell phone.

We are isolating, unpacking the car, and lying awake, worrying. Answering texts, with nothing to say except that we're fine and you should stop worrying. We see no one except each other. Jer and I are alone, together.

I am accustomed to isolation, although I have a reputation for gregariousness. When in 1985 I first was housebound with vertigo, I was alone for most of the day. In the evening,

Jer would come home, go on his run (his sanity exercise), come back, fix some food, tell me a little town gossip, and we would go to bed. I couldn't drive, couldn't socialize, and was miserable as well as ill. In the midst of the illness, I felt deserted by the universe. I missed the daily interactions of work, consulting with colleagues; I felt lost without the pleasures of going out to lunch with friends, going drinking on Friday nights. It was not a good time.

However, as time has passed, the pain of losing a full social life has dissipated. I have grown to appreciate the quiet of solitude and meditation, punctuated occasionally with low-level interactions with friends. But now, during this pandemic, we have lost those ordinary easy encounters, and I'm feeling the horror of isolation all over again.

My surgery has been suspended. I went to Tucson thinking that as soon as we returned, the breast mass would be excised. However, all optional surgeries at the hospital have been cancelled. So we wait.

Part of me feels relief at putting off the operation. It delays the pain and the boredom. But a rational part of me panics, thinking of those cancer cells, increasing every second, changing my body. In isolation, I am beside myself, of two minds, unable to settle in.

The weather, per usual in March, is erratic. The gardens sprout through the mud. Neighbors wave from behind their windows. The cell phone buzzes. Kerri next door brought us a bunch of bananas, leaving them on the porch. Susan Saling is going to paint watercolors and send us photos. I send out Borowitz satires to my progressive friends.

And I continue to write these missives, daily, and am glad to be doing it.

Words are structured and ordered, printed out tidily on paper. If they displease, they can be thrown away. "Art" can go beyond paint and wire and can mean a tidy cupboard and a magnificent casserole, even tulips and muddy earth.

Yer ma,

June (Colleen) Oechler Underwood, born on St. Patrick's day in 1942, turning 78 in this unimaginable year.

Saturday, March 21, 2020
The Tiger Has Claws

Dear Jan,

The pandemic circles us, and my breast cancer surgery has once again been canceled. The receptionist who gave me the news tried to put a good spin on it: I was better off at home than in the hospital; the state has ordered all hospitals to perform only essential surgeries; my age vis-à-vis the virus puts me in a highly vulnerable category. I was better off at home.

This laying out of reasons did not make me cheerful. Dealing with the delay, however, turns out to be rather interesting. I find myself turning to reading, absenting myself in trash novels and murder mysteries, punctuated by Facebook.

Facebook is perhaps not the best way to spend these fear-filled days, although in that weird medium, I can distance myself from my own life. I read my friends' rants against the Trump White House with satisfaction. That satisfaction is definitely not noble, not "good," but there it is.

Still, I am relieved to put off the surgery. This means putting off pain and dependence on Jer. Some tension is relieved. But then, of course, I think of all those ugly cells, reproducing while I'm munching on potato chips. Can't go forward, can't go back: stuck with Donald J. Trump and breast cancer and a pandemic. This is an impressive—and boring—time.

We continue with household chores, and Jer tries to get groceries delivered. Our unease about pantry items exists, although we could live for a couple of months on canned beans and dried rice. But we'd druther live with fresh vegetables, the occasional carrot, saving the cupboard supplies for a different crisis. Did you know that "druther" is short for "I'd rather?"

So, I'd druther not have a medical issue and a pandemic at this moment, thank you. But one does not always get one's druthers. The tiger has decided it's bored and needs to get a taste of flesh. Or even just a little claw into something soft and tender, just to see what the response might be.

Mama

March 25, 2020
Mutterings and Mumblings

Dear Jan,

Like a whole lot of people, I try to distract myself from the awful national news and the ironic cackle of friends who cope by celebrating catastrophes. Yesterday's pandemic sarcasm was "Save Medicare. Let grandma die."

The failure to take care of the oldest, most vulnerable members of our country has resulted in a mountain of satiric essays, take-offs on Swift's 18th century satire about eating Irish babies. I add Saramago's *Death Interrupted* and note that adding grave-digging machines and operators will help the country's economic crises.

That's the kind of distraction that I spent yesterday wallowing in.

Today, after indulging in some unsociable moments, I closed Facebook, photographed the budding tulips, wrote an email to Carolyn Gifford in Chicago who had texted asking how we were doing, opened the studio, and made hot tea.

And I remembered my consoling thought from last evening: I read that those of us who put off surgery are saving scarce medical supplies, especially the Personal Protective Equipment (PPE), for the nurses and doctors treating Covid.

It isn't just that I am too old and feeble for surgery. It isn't that my cancer is unimportant. It is that essential medical people desperately need scarce gowns and masks; I can wait until their emergency needs have abated.

I feel more cheerful; whatever my worries about delaying my cancer surgery, I can see a greater good coming from it. It sounds sanctimonious now that I've written it down, but I still have to say it: I feel better knowing I am helping others stay alive.

Hugs,
Mama

On April 9, I finally underwent surgery to remove the cancerous mass in my left breast. The surgery, postponed and rescheduled four times because of the pandemic, happened suddenly; a small opening in the hospital schedule appeared, and I was at the top of the list.

The Covid precautions meant that the non-Covid quarters of the hospital were bleak and empty. All the Covid precautions were doubled; everyone was heavily masked, and the rooms where I waited had few chairs, too sparse for the size of the rooms. The staff—and surgery requires a lot of medical staff—was grim and efficient—no jokes, forced cheeriness, only eyes seen above face coverings. The oddness was reassuring; strange times called for strange quarters and strange caregivers. I was in, under, and back home in one day, shocked at the speed at which things happened after such long delays.

The surgery, I was told via Zoom, went well. The cancerous mass was removed and looked to be intact, not spreading beyond its well-defined edges. It was also no more difficult to recover from than the earlier biopsy. The follow-up appointments went well, and I found the breast cancer staff to be helpful and affirming. I decided not to have radiation, which was offered as a precaution: my primary care doc as well as my gynecologist agreed with that decision.

I was told that I needed Tamoxifen to reduce my chances of the cancer recurring. I tried it, but the side effects of nausea and dizziness sent me whirling to bed. I then tried a couple other similar medications, with the same result. I imagined a summer, fall, spring, perhaps the rest of my life, fighting nausea, feeling always like I had the flu, and decided against the medications. I would take the upcoming summer's pleasures fully alive; after that, we would see.

My primary care doctor and surgeon were not happy with my decision. Jer approved because he knew of my love of gardening and my need to be outside.

At age 78, I wouldn't have many more summers of smelling the warmed air, the sun on my back, the soil in my hands. I opted for a guaranteed good summer. Had I been 60, the decision would have been different. But I was 78.

And now, in 2023, I have survived for two years, post-surgery. These two summers have been so good that even if the cancer recurs, my deci-sion will have been right. Fingers crossed, no regrets.

And so life—in the middle of a fraught national election, an incom-petent national administration, a pandemic that was killing thousands every day—life went on.

May 22, 2020
A Rainy Friday Evening, in the Midst of a Pandemic

Dear Jan,

Outside, on the Pad, are two Golden Sword yuccas from Portland Nursery.

I had ordered, via phone, a modest yucca from a list of plants found on the nursery's web page. Portland Nursery was not prepared to put out a pandemic catalogue; they did not have the expertise to do full-color photos, nor did they have staff equipped to deal with online customers. My order was taken by a tired-sounding staffer who, I am sure, wanted to be repotting begonias.

When we got to the nursery, it took us a bit to find and nav-igate the pick-up space. We used the designated walkie-talkie to ask for our order, gingerly using an old glove to handle it. And then, to our pick-up space, but staying distanced from the car, a young woman brought a wagon with two three-foot plants, spiky gold and green, whose foliage enlarged the wagon to three times its actual size. We looked puzzled. She frowned. We hesitated.

And then, after a few mutters, Jer and I looked at each other, shrugged, and said to her, "It's fine." Negotiating in a parking lot, shouting to someone 20 feet away, is hard when you are 40; at 78 it's too much. And as I told Jer, there's always room in the garden for one more plant, even a humongous prickly one.

And in the twilight tonight, those spikey green and gold plants make me smile. Cool, gloomy May evenings are made for lime green and golden striped yuccas. These appreciate being released from the confinements of the nursery. They have a view to cheer them up. In a day or so I will lift them from their plastic pots and nestle them into large containers, where they will stretch and preen. The soil will welcome their stringy roots.

An ordinary sort of event—the repotting of a pot-bound nursery plant. But it pleases me tonight to imagine roots gently stretching out, moving around in new welcoming soil. It's like thinking of children, dripping in yellow raincoats, holding out tiny fingers, or cats, stretching in front of the fire. I can dream myself to sleep, thinking of planting, of watering, of watching children and purring cats. The dirt under my fingernails annoys me but also reminds me to be tender toward life, even my own.

And so, a Friday evening in May, cold and rainy, in the midst of a pandemic, with two Golden Sword yuccas outside my studio door, I am content.

Hugs,
Yer mama

May 23, 2020
Pots for the Golden Swords

Dear Jan,

The rain is clearing up, and they say that tomorrow will be benign, the next day balmy, and then it will be hot. It's time to dive into gardens, edit the plants, fill up the holes. It's time to make art—garden art.

The two Golden Sword yuccas got their housing today. I called Little Baja, the pot store, and ordered two terracotta pots, asking for something about 20 inches across and 19 inches deep. They know us at Little Baja; over the years we've bought pots as well as garden decor from them. Their guys winterize our fountain every year. Dylan, the nice young guy on the phone, tried to talk me into coming in and picking them out on site. "Those are big pots," he said. "You might want to look at them first." I refused:

"I'm almost 80 and I am not shopping anywhere these days. Just pick out what you think will work, and we'll bring them home."

And so he did, choosing the pots, wheeling them to the car, and heaving them into the trunk for us. At home, we levered them out and brought them to the pad where the yuccas sit, waiting to be given their new homes. They are big hulking creatures, those two pots, just right for the big honking yuccas.

The yuccas have been made into end stops to the Pad space, serving as frames for the paths to the house. Paintings as well as gardens need frames.

Mama

IV

THE ROAR ON THE OTHER SIDE OF SILENCE

Life can only be understood backwards, but it must be lived forward.
—Soren Kierkegaard

October 25, 2019
The Roar on the Other Side of Silence

Dear Jan,

Last night I was reading a book review in *The New Yorker* in which the reviewer said, "Understanding suffering is an act of imagination."

Yes. I believe that.

I have sometimes thought that I lack imagination. I am not gifted with the kind of empathy you and Jer have. I can bring myself to it, but it doesn't come easily. You are a natural at empathy, and the culture has caught up with you.

Life in the U.S. is gentler now than when I was growing up. We both have been teachers, and good teaching starts with knowing one's students, beginning where they are to bring them along. But you have always known more about your students and incorporated that knowledge more thoroughly into your work than I. You acknowledge others more often and more lovingly than I do.

I have a decent understanding, and extensive knowledge of humanity's suffering. I know the words and actions that mimic empathy, but I feel that I shy away from imagining what the suffering feels like.

George Eliot, in *Middlemarch*, addresses the reader as she describes newlywed Dorothea Brooke, coming to grips with marriage.

Dorothea, on her honeymoon with Casaubon, who is pedantic and emotionally cold, is left alone to experience the sensual and (for her) terrifying art that fills Rome. She breaks down among the weight of suffering and sex she is surrounded with. Eliot says to us, the readers:

"Not that this inward amazement of Dorothea's was anything very exceptional: many souls in their young nudity are tumbled out among incongruities and left to 'find their feet' among them, while their elders go about their business. Nor can I suppose that when Mrs. Casaubon is discovered in a fit of weeping six weeks after her wedding, the situation will be regarded as tragic. Some discouragement, some faintness of heart at the new real future which replaces the imaginary, is not unusual, and we do not expect people to be deeply moved by what is not unusual. That element of tragedy which lies in the very fact of frequency has not yet wrought itself into the coarse emotion of mankind, and perhaps our frames could hardly bear much of it. If we had a keen vision and feeling of all ordinary human life, it would be like hearing the grass grow and the squirrel's heart beat, and we should die of that roar which lies on the other side of silence. As it is, the quickest of us walk about well wadded with stupidity."

"Well wadded with stupidity."

Unable to hear "the grass grow and the squirrel's heart beat [which, if we could,] we should die of that roar which lies on the other side of silence."

Whoa.

Eliot has captured my fear—if I allowed myself to feel as I think I could, and perhaps should, the roar would be unbearable.

Mama

March 19, 2020
Distractions from Distractions

Dear Jan,

Yesterday I reveled in the comfort of the mellowed, fuzzy past; today I am in the murky present. Covid-19 is Here. But it's not "here," in our house or our yard or the studio. Its immediate absence is good, but it can only be held off by constant attention, so we must be always alert. We duck into the street when other people walk toward us on the sidewalk. We avoid exchanging gossip because shouting across the 20-foot distance is too hard. We wash our hands after picking up the newspaper; we scrub the outsides of cereal boxes.

But this constant attention feels vague, unreal. We can't see or touch or smell the virus, yet we obey the official instructions about dealing with its unknowable presence.

There must be words and ways to describe this. Not words describing the economic data of millions unemployed and the national terror of people not having enough food and being unable to pay the rent—we read, in horror and tears, about those conditions. We send checks, too small but something, to charities that pledge to help the worst off.

But still I search for words to describe *our* immediate present, *our* little post-war suburb, where the personal changes have taken place. We are economically stable, food delivery has sprung up, and lots of help has been offered to those of us who are elderly and vulnerable. But the change from cheerful handshakes and hugs to distant waves from the roadway, the absence of anyone just dropping by, the delivery guys who run away after they put food bags on the porch—these are jarring reminders that this time is not normal—not right.

We don't shop to get the big cabbage for the St. Pat's Day dinner. We sit alone, wondering how John and Susan are doing. We wash our hands obsessively. We clean the outsides of bananas and let the mail sit and cure for days.

Each day, I open up the studio, turn up the heat, log onto the computer, bump the radio tuner buttons, and decide whether it's music or news I want to hear. I heat the water in the water pot, and then forget to make tea.

I check my email, then news—*Washington Post* and *The NY Times*. And there's Facebook, the drug of choice that keeps me ratcheted as well as riveted. Facebook allows me to feel like I'm participating in some world other than the studio and house. It's a pretty awful world, but outside myself, and thus a relief.

I've been extra tired and sore, particularly in my arms and legs, since returning from Arizona. Could be psychosomatic. Could be arthritis. Could be cancer. Or some combo of all of the above. Or maybe it's just tension from having to be alert when everything and nothing about me shows code red.

Meanwhile Jer explores how to order food from a delivery service. We get the three boxed dinner kits from Blue Apron on Fridays. And Instacart workers shop for groceries and deliver them to us.

I record all this to try to find language that can make order from this vague, distressing situation, language to describe what is happening here, in this calm suburb. The spaces and houses all look as usual, but the streets are empty. There's no traffic noise, although we live a few blocks from the freeway and are sandwiched between two busy boulevards. It's all a kind of nothingness. Nothing here looks like a crisis. But the crisis is all there is.

Mama

March 31, 2020
Anger, Angst, and Anxiety

Dear Jan,

I started writing these notes to establish something of what it is like to be 77/78 years old, a female, in 21st century America.

The pandemic has changed this writing.

My feelings during these weird and awful days are not much different, I suspect, from what most Americans are feeling—anger, grief, rejection, denial, anxiety, fear—the ancient sorrows of humankind, wrapped into a 21st century way of living in a first-world, white, American, mid-sized city—I am typecast for the occasion.

This evening I have finally moved beyond an anger that stalked me all day. The anger involved politics where mansplaining Sanders bombasts at rallies, while Biden mumbles through incoherent messages. And then of course, the Orange Asshole tweets. Tweets! What a waste of a previously fine word.

I walked my couple of miles alone and thought about my anger. I had targets for my rage, but those targets were not appropriate. Sanders and Biden are being themselves, the political selves they have had forever. Only the Orange Shithead deserves the anger I direct at him, but thinking of him gives me headaches, which is to say, that anger turns back on me.

Not just headaches, but a mid-back ache, like a pulled muscle, that catches me mid-stride, pulling me up and hunching me a bit.

The anger is exhausting. The days are exhausting. Sleep is exhausting.

All of which is to say—I am almost certainly feeling like other Americans—millions and millions and millions. I am luckier than most, but knowing that doesn't help.

I feel better when I respond to other human beings. Waving across the street to the neighbors takes me out of my self-absorption. I like seeing them smile, if only wanly. Each little encounter becomes treasured.

So I find myself letting go of the inward anguish and anger. I go back to observing the crows and robins, the little houses, the empty roads, the angular leafless trees, elegant against the sky. I remind myself to go outside of myself, and observe all that is around me.

This is what I'm saying now, today, at 7:38 PM on March 31, 2020, in my 79th year of life.

Mama

June 7, 2020
A Low-Key Day

Dear Jan,

Friday we drove to Troutdale to pick up a couple of flats of strawberries at the farm stand. This was the furthest we have driven since March 12. The gorge opens up as you drive along the Columbia and the blue Cascade foothills with their mists appear and disappear under the clouds. A good change from our gridded, concrete sidewalks in urban Portland.

The farm stand is wide-open, filled with the smell of fresh vegetables and turned earth. Everyone distances cautiously, but with the kinds of eye gestures that signify good will. The earliest boxes of blueberries have their own space; the spinach is just about gone. We revel in this other life, the life of growing things and people who help the growth.

My writing focuses on these experiences, controlled by age and the virus, while at the same time we are surrounded by other momentous events we can only read about. Downtown Portland is under siege by right-wing thugs and federal and local "law" enforcers who are in cahoots with the Trump mobs. We watch the news, reading of police riots, of weapons held by out-of-town, flag-waving men knocking over 17-year-old women, of tear gas from the official sources, and hours of corralling people to arrest them. Once we were part of rallies and marches to protest the cruel acts of government officialdom. We marched and shouted and swelled the crowds. But now we can't. We are too old. We would put others at risk. We are too vulnerable to the virus. We are of no use in the national or even local crises of democracy. All we can do is continue to live and control what we can.

Control of what we can—cleaning strawberries and making an outdoor space for neighbors to drop by has dampened some of my moral confusion. We wash the mud off the strawberries and set them in colanders to drain. I sneak one, a bit sour and seedy, discarding its green stem in the compost pot. We invite John and Susan over to sit outside and tell tales, giving the neighborhood some life and noise. I make small packets of snacks, carefully washed, so everyone is safe. It isn't enough but it's all we have.

I have sometimes imagined standing in silence, joining a group of 12 women dressed in black, outside a government building, four hours every Friday—but I'll never do it. I can't stand for four hours, I can't join the real protests, the massing of people to confront the police and federal forces; I would be a liability. So I allow myself the fantasy of black-clad women, a few of us, which is in itself quite silly, since it's the sheer numbers of people showing up to protest police killing of Black people that is making the country reevaluate itself.

And so I wonder, even at age 78, how to live the lesser, more comfortable life, and still maintain a moral self.

I tidy my studio, clean the strawberries, write these indifferent musings, vacuum the kitchen, greet the neighbors, watch a kid drawing on the sidewalk, and mumble out my days.

Hugs,
Mama

September 5, 2020
Pain, Recorded

Dear Jan,

The arthritis lurks, making itself known—toes, knees, wrists. Arthritis that just about everyone over age 70 complains about and gets disfigured by. Others' pain; my pain.

Jer has arthritis in his neck which bows his head. His anemia makes him thin and pale. It seems too much.

And then there are the nation's pains. The ugly electioneering. The lies and boasts, the threats and fear-mongering.

The damage of the riots, which strain our civic sense, while homelessness and hunger grow from the pandemic.

I am constantly self-conscious. I laugh too raucously. I forget and step close to friends for a touch on the shoulder or a quick hug. Then I retreat. We all wear masks which muffle voices and hide emotions.

We are lucky. Our pain is muted, not howling. We are not in an ICU bed, nor have we been tear-gassed or threatened by gun-toting Proud Boys. The anxieties that keep us awake are mostly theoretical. Even the bodily failures are just what they are, what they are expected to be at our age, nothing surprising or shocking.

And, the flowers, the gardens, the lilies that surround our communal seating spaces, the tuberous begonias—all lush and beautiful—they are glorious and wild. The soil, well-composted and soft, smells like life itself. Western Oregon is at its most fulsome in September; rose bushes prod us as we walk, perfuming the air. Sunflower heads grow larger and more curious in the lingering dust of the sun.

It's a lovely September evening. Jer and I did a little walk, about half a mile, and my knee pinched but not so much I couldn't finish the walk. A summer of pain juxtaposed against a whole lot of beauty.

Hugs,
Mama

The autumn of 2020, just begun in this last entry, was difficult—harder than waiting for and living through the surgeries or the early days of the pandemic. Early on we thought we were waiting for a change, perhaps a better time. By the autumn it felt as if we were beyond waiting. We were just going on, putting one foot in front of the other, plodding toward an endless horizon. No new stories, no new encounters with friends, no new landscapes to be painted or to evoke joy and surprise. Just one step and then the next.

September 6, 2020
A Hot Afternoon

Dear Jan,

It's a sticky hot afternoon.

Anne Prahl stopped by this morning; we had not seen her for years. Seemingly she hasn't changed, although I'm sure that she has. How could it be—that she would be the same, even after 10 years?

I hear from nearby 82nd Avenue the roar of pick-ups. It's probably a white supremacist rally, horns honking and shouting from the sidewalks. A while back sirens from passing cop cars blasted through intersections.

We are sandwiched between protests at Ventura Park, around 115th, and ones that focused on the east precinct of the Portland Police, at about 45$^{th.}$ We haven't seen any live protesters on 86th Avenue, but last night the helicopters were out, buzzing overhead, and today it sounds like the Proud Boys and their ilk are driving around with their assault weapons.

And here is cheerful Anne, full of funny stories, insights, queries. A sultry afternoon to think about rioters with assault weapons and an old friend's cheerful gossip.

It will be a long autumn, and a longer winter. By the time you get to read this, you will know the arc of the story. You will know if Jer's anemia gets fixed, if Anne Prahl ever shows her age, if this was the beginning or the end of American democracy, or just a muddle through. You will know how it turned out. Or maybe it will just continue. The climate will continue to change, sultry days will always buzz with deadly helicopters, and old friends will show up and sit in the garden to exchange gossip.

Mama

September 28, 2020
Quotidian, Narratives, and Hysteria

Dear Jan,

When I haven't written in a while, notions pile up in my brain. It feels itchy.

"Notions" is the family catchword for ideas not well enough formed to be called "ideas;" it comes from *Middlemarch*, where dithering Mr. Brooke has "notions." He is the one who "went into all that at one time" and has a special place in the U-wood family lingo.

And so, today, the usual stuff, the stuff "we went into," shows up. Right now, tapping this on the keyboard, I am aware of my smooth, tender-skin fingertips; we just finished washing the groceries, and my hands feel the effects.

I have a can of La Croix for a morning treat. Being confined mostly to the property—no travel, no human encounters, no reason for new jeans or shiny shoes—we indulge ourselves: fizzy water instead of flat tap liquid, new plants ordered from on-line, all the colors of phlox and hydrangeas, the smell of lilies and jasmine, the first astonishing tulip display.

Here is Jer back from his walk. The box of bulbs awaits opening, and I have to decide what to plant first, and second, and third. And so goes the quotidian. They say the last warm spell will come later this week, and that will be pleasurable as well as sad. Donald Trump's tax returns have been disinterred, and we are wondering what depreciation he took on his gold-plated toilets. The pandemic grows in strength again, unemployment is up, and people are suffering. And the sun is shining, and we can contemplate new growth this spring. Would we be better human beings if we lived with barren soil, having only milkweed and Russian blackberries for our surrounds? I'm not so sure. Today I am going to plant some asters.

Hugs,
Mama

October 13, 2020
Better Than the News (Or Is This the News?)

Dear Jan,

It's early morning—7:13 AM, and I am already typing in the library. I am not going online, not reading *The Times* or *The Post* or even Facebook.

The house is silent and it's good to slip into the emptiness of a sleeping world. Just me and my tea. I love the absence of everything but me on these mornings. I'm only approximately here—half asleep or lightly alert, not filling the space, not moving the air, just sitting at the laptop table overlooking the Pad outside, moving my fingers and my mind. It's a very still moment.

I am, lightly, reminded of my mother, drinking cold coffee in the still mornings in Pine Station.

It's odd that one would think of this as more still than usual, given that we already live quiet lives. But of course, quiet is always relative. Outside, flocks of birds invade the dogwood to feast on its seeds. They are raucous, and they bounce about until their very movements look like sound. The machinery of the house hums and warbles, refrigerator buzzing, laptop fan spinning. The distant sounds of the freeway begin to get louder.

The automatic coffee maker just snapped to attention, preparing to grind the beans. In a short time, the smell of coffee will fill the house. Jer will be heard, running water and puttering in the bathroom, lights in the dining room will be turned on, curtains put up, the rainy day (it is a gloomy rainy day) will be stared at, as if I could push back the gray and uncover the blue. There is no story in that blue sky, no more than there is in the gray one.

Yer Mom

October 30, 2020
It's Raining

Dear Jan,

It's autumn in Portland. The rain glows on the foliage with spikes of brilliant dying leaves, while purple asters and yellow-gold mums still bloom. Seed heads pop up from lanky gray foliage.

This morning, Jer and I planted the tulips. Jonny, the garden guy who was to do the planting, has disappeared. We were incompatible—he was a maintainer of grass and leaf-blown borders; our gardens resist mechanics. And he knew nothing of tulips.

So Jer and I are digging, slowly, and planting, slowly, and finding that, however much our knees hurt and our heads spin, we can plant—this year. One year, soon, we won't be able to. I wonder how that story will end. It certainly won't involve Jonny. But who will it involve? Will that person be a lover of plants, a designer and artist of growing things? Or a lover of leaf blowers and rototillers?

The rain has come. The elections are next week. The pandemic rages. And Jer will be 80 next October.

Time, the old trickster, keeps gaming our systems.

Cheers,
Mama

This last entry was written on October 30. The next comes from November 18. That means that I did not write on November 4th, 2020, the day of U.S. elections. The day came and has no record here.

I am a progressive American who is appalled by white Christian supremacy and the push for an autocratic form of government. I believe in civic engagement and staying up until the early hours of the morning to get election results. However, anything I could have written about this election pales beside the professional writers at the time—people like Heather Cox Richardson, Jonathan Capehart, and Andy Borowitz—these and many more recorded this dark history better than I. So I wrote—and then deleted—my personal rages at the national situation. Rages, at least mine, about this time were boring, repetitive, incoherent.

Yes, Joe Biden won the presidency in November 2020. Former president Donald J. Trump continues, even after a couple of years, to try to wreak havoc on our Constitution and democratic systems and norms.

We hoped, with the new administration, the pandemic would be dealt with by competent scientists and efficient government systems, and it more or less was; we believed that the country's affairs would return to rational humane decision-makers, as it more or less happened. We continue to hope that science and reason, thoughtfulness and compassion, will govern. My daily writing, my daily existence, continued to focus on dailiness. National affairs affect the tone and subject matter in subtle rather than ranting ways. But the lack of closure about national affairs took its toll.

November 30, 2020
Narratives & Lives

Dear Jan,

Yesterday's Zoom session with you and Jer and Sam was sweet. The four of us start discussions, interrupt each other with silly ideas, slide off into tangentially related thoughts, and enjoy ourselves in peculiar family ways. It all seemed so familiar, so typical and easy-going and fun.

There was, for instance, the discussion of various pronunciations of "Biden" (bye-Den, byDen, baid-n). How one pronounces our President-Elect's name.

The pronunciation question led to digressions of language sounds, like the schwa, that lazy vowel sound (like in "taken") that sometimes finishes off a word with a nod rather than a handshake. The schwa works a bit like novels that wrap up their stories on a trailing-off note—she became a social worker, they married, she became a lawyer, he a dentist—that sort of anti-climactic summary.

I was mulling over trailing-off narratives the other day when I read a column about a soothing TikTok video. TikTok videos are filmed in lengths of a minute or less. The writer of this particular article was admiring a 58-second scene—a bicyclist, wheeling down a country road winding through meadows. For 58 seconds. No beginning. No ending. Just the wheels going swish-swish and meadow weeds left and right—a wide angle view that simply was.

This narrative-less video reminded me (less soothingly) of National Public Radio's Friday feature—short obituaries of people who died of Covid-19. These obits, always featuring five different people, use quotes and visuals provided by families and friends of the dead. NPR edits the materials without adding commentary, merely having Judy Woodruff give the details the family provided while pictures of the deceased, often with family and friends, scroll by the screen. The photos have no text; they simply appear as the narrator's voice overlays them. We search the groupings to identify the person who is being commemorated. Woodruff, the NPR anchor, has a warm delivery but she doesn't drop her voice between one annotated life and another; the names change, the sound goes on in a soft, kindly way, and the stories move along, almost undifferentiated.

It's emotionally moving, and yet disconcerting. The photos come at you rhythmically, one after another. The unpaused stream of voice-over and visuals was an artistic choice—to move from one life to another without pausing, from one eulogized human being—the loving mother, the passionate doctor, the smiling teacher, the motorcycle enthusiast, the kid riding on his Mom's back—to the next; and from one photo to the next—to show us this stream of people who have "passed" with families, activities, smiles, and hugs. They pass by us on our TV set. They are no more; they died of Covid. Their faces are being seen by millions but they themselves lie moldering in their individual graves.

It takes perhaps five minutes to run through all the commemorations. And at the end I want to know (I feel a sense of subdued outrage)— "what was that?" "What am I supposed to do now? Can I mourn for all these—plus the other 265,000 dead? Or is this a morality tale, a *memento mori* of 2020?"

I don't want to think of these as memorials. I want to think of them as stories, as having structures. Yet the only structure is the generalized opening: "Every Friday we…." and the ending "We thank the generosity of the families who shared…" The middle has no exposition, no complication, no exacerbation or explosion or denouement. It's like an endless view of a single stretch of a river, always different, always the same.

It's also a bit like that TikTok bicyclist. Or for that matter, like our discussion of bye-Den, by-din, by-duhn and baid-n, which had no conclusion, only digressions, wavelets of factoids, of interest only to ourselves.

Our jolly Zoom, yesterday, as well as the bicyclist on TikTok and the NPR news "obits", were not shaped as narratives, and yet they served their purposes. Do we need a narrative to find comfort? Perhaps I am wrong to be searching for narrative to enliven this narrative. Is it enough just to observe?

Questions for philosophers or critics. All I can do is observe that these are questions that occur to me. Without answers. Although I do know that the proper pronunciation is "baid-n", whatever my friends might contend.

Mama

January 13, 2021
National Affairs

Dear Jan,

Just as the January light was lengthening, the dark cloud of violence and chaos played out at the US Capitol. It's been one week since the insurrectionists attempted to take over the government while Congress was in session to certify Joe Biden's election as President. The legislators were sitting ducks. The mob of would-be revolutionists fought the police, bludgeoned the guards, and defecated in the halls. They put their feet up on desks and upended file cabinets. They broke windows and statues and showed themselves as malicious vandals.

You know all that, and the outcome—five dead, some Capitol police and Representatives aiding the insurrectionists, the current attempt to convict Donald Trump and remove him from office. Historians have documented these events, so I shan't.

But I was stymied, again, about how to write about national affairs, how to write when I sputtered with rage, cursing the evil one. As you see, I was/am not exactly coherent.

And then I remembered that these notes to you are supposed to be focused on the quotidian of someone in mid-elder-hood.

And so, I return, while facing the trauma of the national events, to my own quotidian. The news confirms that some of our deeply held institutions, like installing legally elected presidents, held. And some are still in doubt. Nothing of the national crisis impacts our daily bread or warm quarters. But the events do affect us.

Last night it rained and blew, a south wind that brought down trees on West Burnside and closed Interstate 84. Flash floods are all around us. But here, up on this knoll on 86th Avenue, the sun shines, the grass gleams wet. It's 50 degrees. The disconnects are stunning.

The rain is great—it's what our greenery thrives on. Yet the mudslides from the forest fires destroy houses and wash away soil. The nightly news feeds our fears. The ugliness of gloating enraged faces preening for videos—set against 50 degrees and sunshine. So many contradictions.

My sleep is disturbed. I lose myself and sink into my unconscious, but in five minutes, I am jolted back into thought. Sometimes I think I have fallen asleep but as soon as my book touches the covers, I'm awake.

In the past I have always loved going to bed. It puts the right punctuation to my days. During the day I am busy—gardening, eating, reading, working on art and the computer, writing to you. Then, come 10 PM, I stop being, stop occupying anyone else's mind or my own productive self. I sink into the comfort of soft blanketing.

In earlier days, Jer and I, incompatible as sleepers, would depart with a kiss as I sleepily headed up the stairs and he drifted off into his downstairs bedroom. But, in these days of insurrection, I have dreaded going upstairs. As I brush my teeth, I resist the thought of resisting sleep. I tell myself that I love going to bed, I love how it warms me. I love it that I can read trash novels. In bed, the arthritis is tamed. The day is done.

But in the aftermath of frantic national scenes, blood and pikes, screaming faces and cries for hanging, I futz around. I brush my teeth twice over. I carefully prepare my electronic devices for overnight charging after I re-check of my email. I consider what books I should carry upstairs with me—will I want to read more about Chaco Canyon? Or perhaps the Paul Bowles' novel about people who are decadent and lack interest in anything but sex and food. Perhaps a *Times Book Review* will carry me to sleep tonight, or maybe Henry Adams and his education.

Finally, I must go upstairs—nightgown on, hair smoothed, pockets emptied, pill containers put aside, downstairs glasses cleaned, socks put on or removed, depending on how cold my feet are—these are the considered motions that a week ago I wouldn't have thought of considering.

I say nothing of this to Jer. He says nothing of his own emotional turmoil. He is reading in bed by the time I have fussed through my prep, and so I go and pinch his toes and rub his calves and we say our final goodnights, each of us feeling alone even while we are together.

After all the chaos and horror and staring at the TV in amazed bewilderment, we have nothing left to say. And so, we double our nighttime rituals, and I go up the stairs, turn on my bed lamp, and face the night.

That's what it's like these days.

Mama

Even now, two or so years after Donald Trump tried to make the country an authoritarian nation with himself as dictator, he dominates our news.

I can't imagine what it must be like for fervent Trump believers, those who swallowed his Kool-Aid and worship his fat angry being. I can't imagine what it is like to be continuously engorged with rage.

I imagine that, because I am a good liberal, a decent human being, I should be able to empathize with people whom we are told are in economic turmoil, who are in the middle of existential anguish, outraged by the sight of women French-kissing and teenagers with nose rings, afraid that their churches will be bombed, and that foreigners will take over their shopping centers. I should understand my fellow elders who live in gated communities and ride golf carts—their knees don't work anymore, and they have been propagandized by fear-mongers.

I do not understand them. I don't want to understand them. I don't want to go into that space full of anger and intolerance and rage and meanness. Even as I know Trump supporters, even as they are sometimes my relatives and friends, I cannot support or tolerate their hatefulness. I refuse to grant them tolerance as they have refused to tolerate me. And I know that this way lies madness.

January 17, 2021
Where Did All the Stories Go?

Dear Jan,

Joan Didion, in *The White Album* from 1968, says, "We tell ourselves stories to live." Didion is sarcastic about the sentimental stories Americans use to hide the truth about their history, but she is also searching for new stories; she believes in stories, but despises tired, misleading myths.

The idea that we need stories, new stories, in order to go on, reverberates for me. At the end of Donald Trump's presidency, much like Didion in those troubled days of 1968, I find myself searching for the right narratives.

Writer Lars Jan, when he was working on a play based on Didion's work, said that her statement: "We tell ourselves stories in order to live," made him feel good about his writing. He felt he was creating meaning, and that empowered him.

"I went through feeling like: I am an artist, and I can create meaning, and that's a source of power...."

Later, he thought the more truthful statement might be: "We create delusions to get by."

He pivots, he says, between the two of them, stories in order to live / delusions to get by.

We create stories; we create delusions. To live? or to get by? To what end do I create stories?

One of my base stories, that I live in a country of "we the people," is being violently questioned. One story braided into my sense of self is that we live in a democracy—flawed terribly, but a place where people like me, from a working-class American family, can aspire to make a better country. This is one of my big stories—ordinary people find their way to living well and doing good.

Stories, for me, have been a way of processing my life, a way toward meaning. And when my life goes askew, doused in racism and insurrection and violence, I find myself story-less. I begin to think I have been living with delusions, set up so I could get by.

The anecdotes I revel in—the sighting of a three-year old in a pink hat or the three chickens named for a trio of singers from the 1940s—don't merely delineate the quotidian, but collectively make the music out of which the society is formed. The pink hat speaks of parenting and its joys and responsibilities and the ability to walk freely around a community that responds in kind to cheerful children and caring and loving mamas. The city-farmed chickens, named and petted, point to a society that has compassion for more than just other humans. And when I see those videos of the storming of the capital by the right-wing militia and white supremacists, living out myths of their own making, I am struck dumb. Making sense of those actions, those people, who have discarded truth, complex and confused as it is, for the simplicities of tribal loyalties, lies, and violence—those stories are alien to me. I struggle today to create a narrative line, even a deluded one, to continue a meaningful life as a citizen in this country I love.

But here is today's quotidian, in its storyless detail: I woke up worrying about whether the coffeepot grinder would work. I drank three cups of fresh brew with my dollop of cream. Jer and I ranted about the ugly characters supporting the insurrection. I googled *The White Album*, just to see what other bits of provocative insights it might carry and found only the quote about creating "delusions," substitutes for "stories."

Voltaire recommended that, at those moments when nothing makes sense, we go home and tend our garden. But it's January. The gardens are hibernating. Only our walks, our dinners, and plant catalogues are available for tending. They will have to do.

Love you,
Mama

January 18, 2021
Dithers

Dear Jan,

We walked to Monti's today to pick up sandwiches for lunch. It was a beautiful day—full of sunlight across fresh-rained lawns, gleaming from last night's drizzle. It should have been a fine January outing. But…

The walk was more difficult than usual. Lots of people were out, so we were often forced to cross dog-poop-filled grassways into the street to avoid other walkers. Drivers were courteous enough, stopping to allow us to cross intersections, even when a minute before they had seemed to speed up. The tiny extra roar of their engines before they slowed left me breathing hard, an internal terror.

Monti's was busy. The Martin Luther King holiday brought more people out than usual, both on the sidewalk and inside the café. The antique store connected to the café was bustling.

People were coming into the café from outside, like ourselves, but also from inside, up the stairs from the main building where antiques are sold. No clear queue or room for distancing existed for paying the cashier; the doors were closed against the chill outside air. I couldn't bring myself to go inside and wait for two or three others to put in their orders in the limited space. And the people coming from inside the antique store had no idea that there might be a line outside for the café, and so they simply got into the obvious queue, ahead of me.

I finally opened the door and stood beside it, the cold air annoying those inside. I tried to explain, got tangled up, was granted a space too close to others, paid for the order we had phoned in, grabbed it, and scuttled through the queue to get outside quickly.

And then I started shaking.

Too many people, too much interaction after having no interactions for so many days. Too many logistical problems, too much activity to sort, masked, unable to read the faces of others or to use the ordinary strategies that smooth our ways through other people's confusions.

I wanted to go home. Which we did, weaving around on-coming pedestrians and thanking drivers for letting us cross. Jer held my hand when things got tense, and I kept my lower lip stiff.

And I realized that something of my ability to navigate the outer world has gone out of me. Perhaps it's merely that I've gotten used to isolation and silence and slow decision making. Or perhaps my slower reflexes and aging brain can't deal with complicated social situations. Or perhaps it's just the pandemic, with its masks and unclear guidelines about how we are to interact and enter closed spaces and make those public niceties that we once used to navigate our ways. Or, most probably, it was all three—unfamiliar territory lacking common sociability rules.

Whatever the cause, I am glad to be back in my quiet studio, door closed, a bit of radio in the background, hot tea, and an all-embracing chair to hold me.

This day too shall pass, and so shall tomorrow. Nothing has occurred except I feel like I've lost something, some joy, some piece of my personal life.

Yer Ma, feeling sad and old,
June

January 21, 2021
Post-Inauguration Mash-up

Dear Jan,

Jer and I and our friends feel today like we might have survived—the country we so love, which seemed to be on the verge of turning into an ugly, violent horror, has a chance to right itself.

There was a "peaceful transfer of power." Such banal words, always part of Americans' smug knowledge of our goodness, turned upside down. We have, as Joe Biden is telling us, returned to a place where truth-telling and decency will be basic principles of our government. And, if he succeeds, the country could become more inclusive, more just, more economically and socially equal. Climate change may be somewhat better managed. More people will have better lives.

Aspirations rather than gains, but at least the aspirations are back. We had been taught the stories about progress, and how ordinary citizens made differences. We accepted ordinary conventions as ordinary—the usual activities—voting and protesting and gathering in communities; we were certain that everyone knew they would bring better lives for everyone. These were our banalities, our truisms, what we knew as truths for so long.

And then those basics of American citizenship were trampled. We began to see how much we relied on the idea that we are a society that tries, however clumsily, to right its wrongs. We almost lost the most basic tenets of our public lives; now we have some hope that we can regain them and that they again will become the norm. And that was what made yesterday's presidential inauguration such a cause for celebration. It restored our national story, a myth that we have always thought we could bring closer to reality.

So how did we spend yesterday, the day Donald Trump left the White House in disgrace, and Joe Biden was inaugurated?

Well, after weeping our way through the Covid Memorial service the night before, we spent the next morning with the inaugural ritual and ceremony: a Black, Asian woman became Vice President of the US; a 78-year-old man was inaugurated during a ceremony that included poetry read by a 22-year-old and the Star Spangled Banner sung by a rock star in a glorious dress—this was the ceremony that we had, in earlier, more innocent years, avoided as too ho-hum to bother with.

We had the Graves over at 11 AM to drink champagne and revel in the joy of the ceremony; we had the Salings at 3 PM for another celebration. We had to forgo the ritual burning of the Trump voodoo doll and mask next door at 9 PM because we were exhausted from the day's socializing, the month's traumas, the four years of panicked outrage. Today neighbor Kerri sent us videos of the event.

And so, right now, all is calm. Our radio station, All Classical, is playing quiet cheerful music and their announcers sound like themselves, soothing and ordinary. Jer has walked. I have edited. We ate breakfast and spoke of Biden's pandemic plans. We have reserved our little house in Oro Valley, Arizona, for winter 2022. And I am looking sideways at some unfinished art, thinking about what it needs.

Life has seemingly returned to normal, through the ceremonies that mark the stories—stories that previously had been too ordinary to speak of.

Long live the stories that allow us to live.

Mama

January 30, 2021
Grandmillennial *Décor*

Dear Jan,

Today's "Homes & Gardens" in *The Oregonian* had advice for millennials on how to "enhance your space for winter." It suggested a "fresh take on 'granny décor.' "

Tra-la. I roll my eyes, irritated at interior decorators falling into the most banal of stereotypes: "Granny." Harumph.

As I happen to be a granny, I take exception to the notion that granny interiors are always "cozy accents, pretty florals, ruffles, and nostalgic throwback details such as needlepoint." This granny (I speak of myself, of course) moved into a post-war ranch-style house and threw out all the whirled and carved furniture from her previous 1900 home. This granny bought light, clean-line furniture to match the unadorned sun that streams through her living room. Needlepoint I never had, nor is it likely that I will. I have walls hung with textile art, but the largest fiber piece bristles with scrunched wire grids that resemble a pointy snail.

But then, other thoughts noodled. I thought about my friends' houses—some of which might fit more closely the writer's stereotyped "granny" category. For one thing, they are full of things, spilling with art and books and objects.

Our friends have created their living spaces differently than we did. "Cozy" in home décor means "lots of stuff." So I could imagine a *Home and Garden* columnist wandering around my friends' rooms, picking up bits of detritus, noting that this silver rabbit or that basket of pinecones would look good in the news photo, accompanying, of course, the needlepoint hanging.

And it's true: rabbits and pine cones do make decent column fodder. But I know these objects and their owners, these "grannies." The rocks in the basket with the pinecones were picked up on their honeymoon, 49 years ago, and the pinecones come from the streamside where the proposal was made. The small bronze rabbits, crafted in Japan, were gifts from their son and daughter-in-law who were married there.

Our closest granny friends are artists. They collect the art of friends. Their walls are stacked with art, magical visions, paintings, prints, textile pieces, drawings—the kind of vibrating walls that interrupt conversation because one's brain can't stop drinking in the art. These walls don't show each piece preciously; the art spills onto every surface, each one having its own form and craft and meaning and story and maker. The visual art echoes with the gatherings that these friends host, where they pull the table into the living room, adding leaves and scooching people together to serve them heaps of crab meat and salad and hot bread. A real granny house, full of stuff, stuff that isn't "cozy" but rather is intimate, evoking lives that have been fully lived.

Another couple, whose walls are somewhat more sparsely populated, have furniture to sink into. Their chairs and couches, spaced for conversation, insist that one subside into them, nursing a hot toddy beside the fire, with the footstool perfectly placed for putting up one's feet. Rows of long-play records and hardcover books live along one long wall. The appetizers are exotic, the conversations well-rounded, questions thought out to make us brainstorm ideas that bound off the titles and are evoked by the labels. A flourish of prairie-style wallpaper dances across the top of the wall, the wood beams are dark, the fireplace crackles with real wood— it's all quite grannyish, warm, cozy, delicious. It echoes their love of music and ideas, of comfort and good food. Unlike our spare front room, meant to showcase the summer sunshine and plants outside, their room is rounded with cuddling fabrics and warm fires and fierce conversation.

However, and here's a confession, while we have the minimalist, light-filled front room, our small back room, gold and buttery, is a different matter. This room which we call the library, was an addition to the house and maintains the same light-filled architecture as the rest of it. It has beautiful hollowed shelves and drawers, a bump-out that extends into the outside. It's just the right size for our big TV. Ah yes, we have a big TV.

It's the library where my granny impulses manifest themselves. In the library, we set up our plush chairs and love seat. The Berber carpet soothes our tired feet; the wooden bookcases between the windows are stuffed with too many, untidily-arranged books. A rocking chair as well as two plump overstuffed recliners take up wall space. The curved coffee table, a bit too large for the space, has a lower shelf that holds piles of art books and brochures, pulled out to show friends. The library has the cactus that our potter friend planted in one of her wonky pots. One side table holds the terracotta bowl that sent three-year-old Sam into uncontrollable giggles because "Mommy, that bowl has feet."

Warm throws are tossed over the mis-matched recliners; a couple of pillows have been plopped down alongside the chairs for those days when our spines require lifting. Those chairs, side by side, face the TV in its elegant nook, in the most conventional granny style. Of course, we didn't mean to make the room a TV room. But it insisted. The hand-crafted TV bump-out looked dumb when I put a single stem of lime-green grass or a scroll with haiku and gingko into it. My minimalism was pretentious. Our TV fit the space perfectly and the recliners sit across from it, right where they need to be. So there we are, Opsy and Grand-mere (Sam's names for us) watching the nightly news on the big screen

"Granny Décor" can't be bought or rendered real in a "Life Section" in the Saturday paper. Granny décor has to be acquired through living. It has to have stories and a bit of dust. It has to be awkward for the space. It has to accommodate long lives, holding smells, tales, and visions both from the past and yet to come. That's why the books about Chaco Canyon and Biosphere 2 sit on the coffee table gathering dust until some evening in February when we start to think about next year's trip to the southwest.

Real granny décor holds future possibilities as well as past lives, the latest novel written up in last Sunday's *Times,* and a new CD featuring Allison Krause. It is aspirational as well as lived. It is both past and present, present and future, charming and messy, absorbing and chaotic. So you see, I've discovered my inner granny décor, while removing all the irritations that the phrase conveyed. Miraculous! And ever-so-granny-like.

Cheers,
Mama

It was a relief to come back to the mundane, the silly, the quotidian. In the midst of national trauma, I needed something of my "real" life—days composed of notions and ideas, scenes and stories. Life, as we knew it, was still around.

February 15, 2021
The Icy Burden

Dear Jan,

Yesterday's exhilaration has turned to today's dismay, as we see that the trees and bushes that were intact and glowing last evening have this morning an inch or more of ice, bowing them down, menacing whatever stands underneath. Not a bird nor squirrel nor human is out. The whole world is holding its breath, hoping that the largest bough, fat with cold slabs, won't break through the lower branches, bringing them down.

Our beloved ash tree has already lost good-sized limbs. The street below it is blocked with downed branches. David's truck, next door, is covered by a sprawling branch; its tires are mired in frozen slush. As we watch, more limbs, more ice, more crashing sounds, slabs of tree and ice from the wires plummeting and impaling themselves in the iced snow below. The sounds are unceasing.

And then slowly, the temperatures rise. Jer starts to shovel the sidewalk; David comes by with his own snow shovel. He does the driveway while I peck away at the walk, and then he finishes that for me, too. These neighborly friends know about kinwork, much to our relief.

We have an appointment for the first Covid-19 vaccine on Wednesday, and we need to get there safely. If we can navigate the shoveled driveway, we will be free.

So, the crystals turned to ice slabs overnight and the delight in the light and sparkles turned to shudders as ice spears rained down. The changes come at us, fast, slow, welcomed, and endured.

Mama

February 17, 2021
Vaccination Day

Dear Jan,

I keep feeling that getting the Covid-19 vaccination will change my world. It won't, of course. The iced up roads will still be here, people will still be dying because of the deep freeze. Corruption in government and climate-change deniers will still make news headlines, and Pfizer's magic shot won't make my aging body and nervous system any younger. Nevertheless, it feels important to me. It is important. Yes.

I found that the last week has emphasized my own frailties in ways I have been denying. Specifically, shoveling snow not only revealed weak muscles, but also that something has changed in my compromised vestibular system. I was made dizzy long before I got sore muscles. I never made it to the blistered hands point of shoveling.

But beyond that, I felt out of control, wobbly on foot, and terrorized in mind. The iced-up world, even as we were warm and cozy, even as it was beautiful and serene, sent all my systems—emotional, temperamental, physical—into tizzies.

I did all the important things that needed done and even shoveled on both Monday and Tuesday. But there was an underlying taste of fear.

Today we go to the Safeway on 69th and Sandy to get our Covid shot. Getting the appointment was a coup; we are among the first of our peers here to have access to the vaccine. The driveway is clear. By 5 PM, home from getting the shot, we will have stopped rehearsing the way to Safeway, the papers we need, the masks, the IDs, all the things that we have been fussing over.

But early today, I see myself as a twittering, finger-flapping old lady, someone who can't quite hold it together. It's not an identity I ever imagined I would have. But here I am; the world outside is there. We'll see how it goes.

Mama

February 21, 2021
Innoculated

Dear Jan,

We are inoculated. First shot of Covid-19 vaccine.

It was chaotic. It was fraught. It was not all that nice. But it is done, and we are good. We are more than good; we are feeling secure.

The Safeway vaccine site was insane. The snow and ice had kept people from buying food for almost a week, so everyone was there. Parking lot madness; store interior frantic. June, befuddled.

No one knew where the shots were to be given. No one cared. The freeze had caused a pipe to burst inside the store; the worst damage was covered with plastic sheets, with shelving pushed at odd angles around the area. The pharmacy, located at the furthest reaches, had a line waiting for med refills, non-distanced because there was no room; the waiting room for shots, off to one side, was the size of a walk-in closet.

Chatting with the people inside the waiting room was half pleasant, half crazy-making because it was small and dim and deserted except for the three of us making small talk behind our doubled masks. It was a long time before anyone noticed we were there.

And yet it worked. Despite the dirt, the confusion, the insecurity of Covid safety measures, I got my vaccination; Jer got his vaccination. Our arms were nicely sore, not bad. We doubt that we caught Covid during the outing.

And so, today another chunk of anxiety has fallen off. We get the second shot in March, on my birthday, when pansies and primrose, crocuses, and daffs bloom. It will happen.

Mama

V

PINE STATION, PENNSYLVANIA: THE CLAN

Nothing you do can stop times unfolding. / You don't ever let go of the thread. —William Stafford

September 22, 2019
Stories from the Clan

Dear Jan,

It's been a while since I last wrote. And that's because you and I spent five days together, flying to South Carolina to visit your aunt and my sister, Mary, at the home of her son, Jeff.

When I was a teenager, my sister Carol was closest to me in age, and we engaged in sibling rivalry; Mary was younger and didn't pose a threat. I was old enough to hold her in my lap and feel grown up. Mary babysat you when she was 15; she lived with us for a semester in her sophomore year in college. Thus, when I learned that Mary was ill, I needed to visit her. So Jan, you and I made the trip. We abandoned Jer home alone, knowing that his anxiety would still be thumping away. Kinwork vs.kinwork. But we had to go.

On the plane we were a mother-daughter pair, laughing and talking, enjoying a chance to be together. At Mary's bedside though, we sat apart, becoming her audience, meant to listen, chuckle, and agree. We were gathered around the controlling storyteller, paying homage to her—and ultimately to my clan.

You didn't spend much time with my Pennsylvania country clan and coming to it from city life on the West Coast, you seemed a bit dumbfounded. Even I found it startling, seeing Mary from her command post in her bed, with the pillows piled behind her, treating her oxygen nose pads with disdain. She carried on as if we were pilgrims, come to sit at her feet and hear her wisdom. Her children and grandchildren and friends of relatives of in-laws, invited to visit with the out-of-towners, also gathered around, encouraging her. Mary appeared, even in her sickbed, full of energy, full of stories.

By the time she was 15, Mary was the storyteller of our generation. She and my dad, your grandfather Pap-Pap, could hold a dinner table, a bar room, a group around a campfire, spellbound, with mock suspense that twisted around to provoke hoots of glee. The stories were often self-deprecating—Mary, riding with the Hell's Angels in the late 60s; forcing the UPS to hire women in the 70s; leading rambunctious Girl Scouts through briar-filled thickets in the 80s.

I tried to tell stories too, but I was never as good as Mary and Dad. They were the champs.

Mary's current physical state—her COPD and near blindness—and her rejection of our other siblings—couldn't be denied. Except deny it she did, refusing to acknowledge any of it. She never spoke of her health or the tensions between her and others in the family. She simply told stories.

It was as if she rehearsed her stories, her shaped memories and observations, before we got there. She has a sharp memory, a sharp tongue, and a stubborn nature. We learned of her decision not to fight death but to go as she lived, mocking the world, reading with her magnifying glass and Kindle and large monitor, drinking coffee and listening to the South Carolina birds from her windows. And telling stories.

Mary revealed an important piece of her strategy when she told us we should watch Ken Burns' *Country Music* series on PBS. My whole generation grew up on country music, "Hillbilly" music, we called it. Minnie Pearl and the Carter Family were part of our Saturday entertainment. I played the accordion. CJ, your now-deceased Uncle CJ, sang Hank Williams and Johnny Cash with me in junior high, and later by himself with his guitar, at the bars and campfires he frequented. His kids and grandkids carry on the tradition. In Wyoming, even Jer, a slightly more sophisticated townie, was briefly part of a bluegrass band.

That music and its lyrics are embedded in my psyche, and in Mary, also. Now, these many years later, those country songs seem to me as formal and mannered as any opera. But as the narrator of the documentary says repeatedly, the songs were country folks' expression of emotions too difficult to speak of directly. The songs tell stories—you know the drill—of pain, heartache, home, men, mama, drinking, death.

Mary told the story, known by everyone at the gathering around her bed except us, of arranging for the gravestone of her deceased husband, Harold. When Harold was dying, Mary traveled north from South Carolina to north-central Pennsylvania, where she found a hilltop cemetery beside a country church. She decided Harold would be buried there and bought a plot for him. On that same trip, she consulted with an old Pennsylvania stonecutter, Mr. Warner, for the text and décor of the headstone, to be delivered to the church when it was finished.

After Harold's death, after the stone had been carved and approved of, about three months after everything seemed settled, Mary, in her bed in South Carolina, got a call from Mr. Warner, in Pennsylvania. The necessary pleasantries were exchanged—how are your children, how's the weather down south there, is the huntin' any good this year?—and then Mr. Warner came around to the purpose of his call:

"Um, Mary, um, the stone is all set up and in place, looks real good, faces out at the mountains just like you said, but we were wondering, the church people and us, we just got to thinking and wondering—and of course we called some mortuaries and what not around the county—but the church folk, well they told me, well, they said I should call you—we were wondering, um, um" [insert more ums and hems and haws]—

"Where's your husband?"

Mary, turning in her bed to look at the stand where the urn with its ashes sat, said lightly, "Why, Mr. Warner, he's right here beside me."

The anecdote would make a fine honky-tonk ballad.

I keep returning to that carefully crafted story, how Mary evoked the confusion of the church people, waiting for a body to be delivered, while the family in South Carolina thought all that was over with. I am seeing the formality of her tale, how she takes chaos of dying and death, of pain and sickness, of the logistics of cremation and mortuaries, and the presence of a living clan, and turns them into a story that sent her audience, sitting around her bed, into raucous laughter.

That's what country music is so good at—controlling emotions that don't fit into ordinary conversation. Storytelling is the non-musical version of this tradition. That's what Mary meant when she said that her education had been through country music. My family's way of dealing with tough emotions was always through storytelling, crafted like ballads and wailing heartache songs. Mary absorbed and perfected that education.

Mary is a Pennsylvania hillbilly transplanted to South Carolina. And I'm a wine-drinking Prius driver, 3,000 miles from "home." I say "interested," not "innerested," I listen to NPR and classical opera. Yet, as you, Jan, note, as soon as I start talking about family, my voice takes on a twang and gets a bit higher and more nasal—not a lot, certainly not so's I would notice—but there it is. I tell stories, inadequately but with a certain pleasure.

And here you are, Jan, yourself a novelist and essayist. The turning of chaos and emotion into tolerable shapes is carried on. The line, from the laughter around the family supper table, through the Mary clan gathered around her bed, to your books and thoughts, is gathered on our bookshelves.

June

Oct 15, 2019
Continuities

Dear Jan,

When you were a small child, my gardens mostly failed. I grew hundreds of violets in Wyoming, but nothing else. In your teenage years in Kansas, the gumbo of eastern Kansas soil defeated me. My compost heap there, which smelled good and was crumbly and rich in hand, never loosened the clay. My flowers died, year after year, encased in the strangling soil.

In our first residences in Portland, the shadows and roots of the yard trees defeated me. Only in our last move, to this sunny ridge, have the gardens become consistently gorgeous.

Our current city blooms were fertilized by my learning from prior failures. Compost now amends the soil and holds the clay at bay. Earthworms wiggle and make spaces for roots. Flowers, expected and unexpected, pop up at all seasons; I plant recklessly, knowing that someday soon, they will dance in the wind and bring color to the neighborhood.

If you want to know, then, some of the possibilities of elderhood, I present you with the stories of my gardens. As a young adult, working, raising a child, networking, teaching, and writing, these used up all my mental and physical space. Now, as an elder, I can plant, connect with the earth, and slowly grow a beautiful space.

Love,
Mama

August 15, 2019
Music, and Poetry, and Memory,

Dear Jan,

Sometimes I imagine that we didn't teach you enough, didn't insist that you read the best that's been thought and taught in the world, and that we ignored Sunday School where you would have imbibed King James rhythms with your cookies. However, I realized today that heavenly music and glorious poetry are actually large parts of our mutual history.

The music that I first thought of was opera, which I started listening to when I was 38 or so. We were living in Kansas. In 1980 I attended an eight-week seminar at the University of Kansas where I met Carolyn, my life-long friend, who had me listen to the Jussi Bjorling duet from the *Pearl Fishers*. That hooked me. I began listening, over and over, to every opera I could buy in Emporia, Kansas. It wasn't easy in those days, no online services, no easy deliveries of CDs. But we found an opera-of-the-month club to join, and as each long-play record appeared in the mail, I played it, over and over. I wanted to learn the lyrics, know how the words tangled with the music, what the tropes were in the 19th century and how they changed in the 20th. I came around to listening to the Metropolitan Opera on Saturday mornings on the radio.

The house at 901 Rural had an architecture that was made for loud, 19th century opera—the sprawling wrap-around porch with three doors and six windows, opening into the two Victorian parlors with the velvet couch and high-backed chairs and tall stereo speakers. You and your high school friends would come and go, making sardonic remarks about the "noise." You wandered through the back parlor allowing screen doors to slam and ate apples and sat on the porch with Tanya and Delaine and Anne. The music from our speakers, I am told, percolated into your bodies, booming and soaring, as well as annoying, teasing, and taunting.

Today I was listening to Chopin's variations on Mozart's *Don Giovanni*, a big piano piece backed by a quiet orchestra. I imagine Chopin remembering Don Giovanni's aria, just as I am remembering opera in Emporia, Kansas, on warm summer evenings.

You and I have different musical tastes—you hated Johnny Cash, who I insisted on singing along with. I'm not sure if you remember the bluegrass band in Laramie (you were two and three and four when we lived there), but I remember one evening when we were having a noisy party and you appeared, sleepy in your nightgown, and I picked you up and we stood and swayed and danced a little while the guys picked and fiddled and vocalized and our friends chatted and drank, a pod of warm-smells and happy sounds in the cold high desert.

And you played the piano. Played it a lot. Seemed to really enjoy it and to want to play it well. As a kid I took piano lessons, but in front of others I was always overcome by self-consciousness. My father played the piano like a clarinet (jazz riffs from the 30s and 40s) and I drove him crazy when I practiced, trying to find notes while always losing time. I never overcame his voice in my head, counting out the measures, while I stumbled around the keyboard.

Did we sing together when we rode on our various trips? I remember the trip to Pennsylvania, from Kansas, when you were, um, 16 probably, because you could drive. The trip was many miles long, across half the continent, and so we memorized poetry. The poem I remember best from that trip was Yeats' "For Anne Gregory"

> "Never shall a young man,
> Thrown into despair
> By those great honey-coloured
> Ramparts at your ear,
> Love you for yourself alone
> And not your yellow hair.
> ....
> "I heard an old religious man
> But yesternight declare
> That he had found a text to prove
> That only God, my dear,
> Could love you for yourself alone
> And not your yellow hair."

Neither of us had honey-colored hair, but somehow the rhythms and rhymes of this silly poem has stuck with both of us, throwing feminism and self-esteem out the window, all for the art (or artlessness) of the language and rhymes.

I have been thinking about poetry a lot these days, riding with you along the vast fields of the Midwest, reciting, re-reciting, reminding each other of lines and then reciting again, the poems that we choose to memorize. When you were a tyke, we looked for cows out the windows, but as a teenager you went for poetry.

I have phrases from poetry that bounce around in my head: "They strayed, impassioned, through the littering leaves." "To strive, to seek, to find, and not to yield." "Ah love, let us be true to one another." "It was a beauteous evening, calm and free." And at this season of fruity-ness, "Do I dare to eat a peach?" And of course, there are the semi-memorized lines, like others in Eliot's *Prufrock*: "I will walk along the beach. I will wear my trousers rolled. I hear the mermaids singing, each to each: I do not think they will sing to me."

Poetry, even in these isolated bits, comes with a sense that is larger than the words. I remember you looking at me with total bafflement when I recited the "littering leaves" lines. I too am bemused by the feeling, incomplete sex, sweet melancholy, that they evoke in me. Without the whole poem, without the line in context, the feeling is inchoate, yet it lingers, yearning, alone while together.

I suspect that lines of music, like bits of poetry for me, linger with you, acquired during those adolescent days of popcorn and apples on the porch while opera blasted from inside. You would recognize the *Don Giovanni* duet if you heard it, even if you couldn't name it. Both of us can sing a phrase or two of the ballroom scene of Verdi's *La Traviata*. The mingling of music and memory, of poetry and memory, is strong and shared by both of us, communion with the greats while the lessers listen.

"Was it a vision or a waking dream? Do I wake or sleep?" Am I only imagining that opera and Johnny Cash and Yeats and Keats and Eliot have provided us with a bond as deep as any Biblical training? I had King James; you did not. But you can sing *Traviata* in Italian; I can only hum it.

I'll leave you with another Yeats: "Oh chestnut tree, … Are you the leaf, the blossom, or the bole. / O body swayed to music, O brightening glance, / How can we know the dancer from the dance?"

A poem should not mean but be. A daughter should not be examined but loved.

Mama

A moment of experiencing music in the present, which is what I was doing on that mid-August day, swelled into the memories that took over the writing. Those memories get tied to the mother-daughter bond that these writings are a continuation of.

I've always said that if I believed in a god, it would be because of music. And shared music. And shared poetry. Common beauty. Common ecstasy.

The responsibility of parents for training and nurturing their children is sometimes too vast to bear. Always there is the possibility of doing more. And so it's a relief to remember that even if I ignored Sunday School, I instilled music and poetry in your brain. Whew!

Tuesday, March 17, 2020
My 78ᵗʰ birthday

Dear Jan,

I woke this morning to start the 79th year of my life. And I am wondering—what pieces of myself have I retained over the years? Do threads of my earliest life still twine around my bones, my arms and eyes, my brain and heart?

Back in the late 1940s and 50s, I was part of a large family, but also a solitary child of woods and water. We lived in Pine Station, Pennsylvania. Pine started as a logging camp in the late 1890s. The mountain was logged, and the Susquehanna River was the highway that took those logs to market. The village housed loggers and river workers. However, by the 1940s and 50s, most signs of its old industry had disappeared. It was a hamlet on the edge of a second-growth forest, with 15 or so houses, where everyone knew everyone else.

My parents, both from large families, fed and bathed and provided beds for all kinds of relatives and friends. People showed up, kids tagging along, stayed for supper, and left a week or two later. Some relatives stayed the whole summer. My immediate family consisted of five kids three or four years apart. As one among an ever-changing batch of kids, some siblings, some cousins, some children of friends, I had the freedom of not being noticed. None of the others were my age, so I had hours alone, exploring along the river and up the mountainside, pretending to be an army scout or a native American, hiding behind trees, ambushing squirrels and robins.

I remember running, running, running, rain pelting and sun beaming on my bare skin. I still can feel my toes on the rank-smelling asphalt road, sinking into the soft tar. I would duck under pine trees flinging myself down on their needle-strewn dirt; pick my way through tough bushes; and then plunge my feet into the tiny run, the creek that tumbled rocks into smooth rounds. I hid, from nothing at all, behind trees and within roots, smelling damp earth, playing at invisibility.

And I was blessedly alone. Home was noisy and chaotic, full of diaper smells and smoking adults and bawling toddlers. In the house, I sneaked unnoticed to my dusty bedroom where I ate green apples and grapes and read Nancy Drew mysteries. I was indulged—the cheerful, nondescript girl, one who mostly did her chores and never talked back. Being the "easy" one meant no one worried about me. That meant I had freedom.

At age 10, my travels included hiking through the woods near the one-lane, paved road that ran up Pine Mountain. The road zigzagged through our 67-person hamlet, across the tracks, and up the mountainside. Pine Mountain, whose banks at that time were filled with laurel, second-and-third growth pines, dogwood, and weedy maples, rose above the New York Central train tracks that followed the river. The river consisted of pungent mudflats and polluted water. Pine Station huddled between the mountain and the river. I explored it all.

I meandered down the slopes to the Susquehanna through the weeds and spindly trees and low bushes to the watery muck. Skunk cabbage grew everywhere, and mud oozed through my toes. Every spring, I re-found the secret meadow of wild violets and lily-of-the-valley clusters. On the mountainside, I knew where teaberries hid themselves and huckleberry bushes littered the banks of old logging roads. I could identify birch limbs—the ones to be gnawed on when I was pretending to be a woodsman. Sometimes I spied on people who didn't notice I existed.

Back at the house, I sat in corners, listening to grown-up conversation, not understanding all of what was being said but basking in the rhythms of women's voices, the way they talked about Jacob and Mrs. Burnham and the Gardners and how that guy smacked Jeannie around and the tiresome business of growing cabbages. They talked about cleaning up sticky messes from canning and seeing mouse droppings in the cupboard and a lot about family, step-cousins and second wives. Talked and talked, while I colored in coloring books, or sat under the table, munching on dry bread.

I always wanted to be invisible, to find out what it was like to be someone else. An older girl, Kate Henley, who was in high school and much too old to be my friend, lived across the road in a big old coffee-smelling house. Kate, blonde, blue-eyed and timid, was exotic for me because of her string of boy friends who showed up with hotrods. I wanted a boyfriend with a hotrod but didn't want to have Kate's ugly father. My father was tall and handsome and boisterous and cheerful. Then there was Joyce Lingle, a couple of years younger than I, whose house didn't have running water. I stayed overnight with her once in a while, and she had a chamber pot under her bed. I think I used that thunder mug once, just to see what it was like. I can still feel its cold porcelain rim on my skinny behind.

I spent a lot of time brooding in the one-room Methodist church, whose doors were never locked. Although I didn't realize it until much later, it was my aesthetic model as well as my moral mentor. It was a spare and open place, with ceilings that were higher than our whole house. It had rhythmically-placed, satin-shiny wooden pews, and arched, opaque, luminous windows that reached the ceiling. It was clean and open and uncluttered, the exact opposite of our house, which was always a hive of dirt and kids and food and people, a clutter where I could hang out, eat green apples, leave their cores on the side tables and prints of my muddy feet on the couch. I loved both the spare, clean-lit church and the chaotic disarray of home. Both returned that love, in different ways.

I was required to help my mother, but she was not a heavy taskmaster, liking to have time to herself, even if it was only while she was doing dishes or ironing. I could slip out on her or tease her to let me go, promising to do the work later. Mostly she did the work herself, but I put in enough time that I was seen as "good."

I knew I was never actually "good," although I had long periods of time when I wanted to be. My parents had strong views of ethical behavior, mostly imposed on themselves. Taking care of family, watching out for the vulnerable, being responsible citizens and volunteering in the community, paying one's debts—all the traditional values were modeled and gently insisted upon. My mother took us to the tiny Methodist church, where I learned to sing "red and yellow, black and white / all are precious in his sight…." I knew I couldn't live up to the standards of church and books, but I wanted to try. Maybe, I thought, I'd try out for a nunnery (whatever that meant to the social Methodism I was part of) or become a teacher who does everything for her students while demanding their absolute obedience.

To be good was confusing to me, because, as a reader of Victorian children's literature, I knew a lot about "good" people. They didn't drink or smoke. They had children whom they loved and who might be naughty but who loved them back. Romances were resolved in marriage. Everyone was white and well-mannered and well-spoken. But I lived with real people, and they weren't good like the people in the books. They didn't speak in full sentences, gravely, pronouncing wisely on small children's mistakes. Both my parents smoked. The Lingles, Joyce's parents, drank beer; Mr. Lingle once gave me a teaspoon of whiskey for my sore throat. My parents also drank beer and had a bottle of whiskey in the cupboard beside the stove.

Once I asked my mom how the Lingles could go to church and still drink whiskey, because going to church was supposed to make them good people. My mother laughed and laughed and then said that she and my dad drank beer and weren't we good people? Almost certainly I nodded yes, but still pondered the question of goodness off and on for years.

Yes, I was naïve about what being good meant—I still am, even after 78 years. I give people leeway, but in my heart of hearts, I judge—myself harder than others, but I judge, nevertheless. The conventional books of the era told me what "good" was, and, although I am no longer a Methodist, I absorbed just enough of those ethics to have remnants hanging around. Maybe those voices I heard—women around the table—also retained their power to speak to goodness. They condemned violence, were tolerant of what was then seen as "immorality" (i.e.: sexual misdeeds) and horrified at poverty and hunger. They were indignant at injustice, although mostly ignorant of the horrors of the greater world. Reading, daydreaming in the silence of a beautiful space, listening to my elders—all these formed my ideas of how to live my life, on my own terms, but always aware of the rest of the world as it existed outside me.

And so, it's the beginning of my 79th year, having, on this very day, shed 78 years of my life. I drink beer and wine and whiskey and I still try to be good and I still want to know more about people. I am still sly and cheerful, and I still like gobbling huckleberries and playing in oozing mud.

Mama

Watching the crows at our fountain reminds me of a continuity from then to now. Our city crows are an unceasing source of entertainment. They are larger than the fountain's concrete basin; their black wings hang over its sides. They start their bathing by standing, sleek and formidable, looking over the gardens, checking for cats and squirrels. They then step into the ring of water. Raising their wings, they begin to splash. Suddenly they are puffy and fat and foolish, their pinfeathers raised and their wings wet and askew.

This morning, in looking at the crow preening at the fountain's edge, I remembered playing in the hose, back in Pine Station, when I was a kid. We had no shower in our house while I was growing up. But the hose, with its fat arc of water, could be stepped into and I could shake the water all over my hot skin, sweating from the summer sun. As I remember it, that was the closest I ever came to feeling bird-kin, shaking the water and dancing through it, forming rainbows in the sun.

Writing about ailments is boring. It's much more fun to watch the resident crows bathing outside our window and remember the sensation of hot sunny days and cold arching water through which my seven-year-old body could expand its tiny self and be kin with sleek black flying royalty.

August 3, 2020
The Nubbin

Dear Jan,

A few days ago, in a book review, the reviewer said that the author had found the nub, the tiny grain of sand, around which a character had coalesced.

It's an old idea, of course, that we have a core that remains stable through time and a variety of environments. Lots of people argue against this idea—we slough our skins every seven years, we make and remake ourselves, it's never too late to change, etc.

I find myself wondering if I have any core left from my earliest experiences.

Lying awake during one of my 3 AM hot flashes, I thought of scenes from my 70-odd years. I remember, from age two or three, lurking, watching from behind a tree as neighbors hoed their gardens and yelled at their children.

I was always a watcher, on the edge of landscape and people, wondering how others lived, noticing how people talked about other people.

The talk was not always kind. Mrs. Burnham's oldest son, Bobby, was, as we said, "slow," "weird" to us in that country community. It was Bobby that my mother feared had made off with me when I disappeared one summer afternoon at the age of three. I remember coming into the kitchen off the back porch, where I had been asleep under a tarp. The kitchen was full of adults—legs and bellies to a three-year old—moving around, loud and accusing and frightened. The neighborhood search for me was being organized. My mother was screaming at Mrs. Burnham, accusing Bobby of—well, mothers' imaginations are wide and deep, and a lost child is terrifying, and the prejudices among country folk in the 1940s were just below the surface.

Mrs. Burnham and my mother were equally stubborn and disliked one another, perhaps a dislike that had its beginnings in my mother's accusations. The Burnham family lived in the old train station by the railroad tracks. Their property, a weedy field, ran out to the paved, narrow village road. I don't remember a Mr. Burnham, although there were enough children that there was such a person.

Up the road from our house was a barn; it faced a big field and behind it was the corn patch and fields where the pigs and cows were allowed to roam. The farmer, I will call him Charley Roadman, lived in that barn, along with many children and dogs and, at night and in the winter, with the cows and pigs. He had a child by one of his girls when she was 13 or so. Charley Roadman was sometimes found sitting outside the barn/house on a broken chair, taking potshots at puppies, perhaps because they ate too much and were a nuisance, or maybe just because he needed some entertainment.

Charley Roadman was our nearest neighbor up the road. I had to walk by the barn from the school bus to home when I was in first grade, and I was terrified. The dogs would come out and bark, and Charley could be ugly-mean.

On the other side of us, in the last house before the road started up Pine Mountain, lived the Hortons. Their house was a one-story shack. They had no indoor plumbing, and the Mrs. was enormous. Our childhood joke was that she had to back into the outhouse because she was too big to turn around in it.

But the Hortons had fruit trees in their yard just on the other side of our garage, and we stole their peaches whenever we thought we could get away with it. They surely knew we were poaching, but I don't remember anyone getting into trouble for it.

I also don't remember the male Horton, but I remember vividly the awful Charley Roadman.

Across the road from us were the Henleys. Adele Henley was one of my mother's good friends, and I spent a lot of time at that house, which was on a large piece of land along the railroad. Across from their house was Pine Run, the stream that ran under the little culvert and down along the length of our narrow property, through the swamp and bottomland fields beyond, to the Susquehanna River.

I remember that our dining room looked out toward the river, and Charley's fields, and that scene seems always to be bathed in a golden light: my young mother and father, three kids full of potential and mischief, good food, a golden haze that surrounded our house and made it safe. That safety and its globe of goodness has stuck with me for many years. A nubbin of watching as well as feeling, not shared with anyone, just as I observed that Charley Roadman was a horrible man, of whom no one spoke.

I know there were 67 people in that hamlet—I could count them, one at a time, so I must have known how many kids Charley Roadman had. And Mrs. Burnham. The Henleys had four, and John Henley was a hard man. I remember Kate Henley coming to our house with a bloody face and a panicked crying. She had been riding her bicycle down the hill from the railroad tracks, where the Pine Mountain Road went up Pine Mountain. We all loved and feared riding down that hill because you could get going really fast. A slight curve meant you had to have control of the bike, and we all had had regular wipe-outs.

This time, Kate took a header off the bike and appeared, dripping blood from a cut on her head, terrified. The blood didn't bother her (we were always scabbed up and messy from falls and bumps and accidents). But she had broken a spoke and was terrified that her father would find out. "Daddy will hit me, daddy will hit me." I can't see her face but can hear the words, which she kept crying as my mother tried to clean up her bloody face.

What happened after that I don't know—I hope that my dad fixed the bike and John Henley never knew that Kate had mangled it in that exhilarating zoom down Pine Mountain.

The Henley boys had a streak of cruelty in them; they loved terrorizing Halloweeners (like us) who loved being terrorized. They rode up and down the road on Halloween night with guns, shooting them at intervals. They almost certainly knew where we were and didn't actually shoot *at* us, but the cruelty was in power they exercised during those dark nights. I remember lying in the ditch, watching headlights. I heard men in trucks, laughing, hanging out the windows, searching for us with those blinding spotlights.

Other pieces of early memories still resonate with me. I remember my mother and her friends, Biz and Adele, talking about their lives, making jelly, their neighbors, the awful Charley Roadman and his daughter, neighborhood kids whose ailments were interesting if only because there were so many—impetigo, measles, mumps, chicken pox, lice.

The strongest memory of a childhood ailment that I have was of a sinus infection. I got to lie in bed and watch my mother work in the kitchen through the open door. It's another golden vision, because she was doing her morning chores, humming to herself, the bed was warm, and I had her to myself, my brothers at school. I could watch her work, totally safe.

I have another memory of watching her in a different house, early in the morning, before anyone else got up—school mornings, when she was the first person to get up.

My mother was irritable on those mornings, having to get up earlier than anyone else, moving silently through the cold, damp house. She would go to the basement, shake down the furnace ashes and build up the fire. Back in the kitchen, she made sack lunches for six people, and pried everyone out of bed, everyone who hated getting up and blamed her and made her nag them to get ready to catch the bus. She had to get out the breakfast cereal for the kids and fry the bacon and eggs and toast for Daddy. But before that, when it was still dark out, cold winter dawn showing through the windows, after she had gotten the fire going and the heat coming out of the registers, she allowed herself a few minutes, perched on a stool between the stove and supporting wall, to drink cold coffee and smoke a cigarette, observed by a small girl, who sat, with heat rising from the radiator, and warmed her bottom parts.

That nubbin of a moment in the life of the watcher.

Love you,
Mama

August 4, 2020
Goat Hill and the School in Town

Dear Jan,

My early life, as I remember it, was a mix of loving warmth within the family and terrifying people and inadequate institutions outside it.

The first school I attended was Goat Hill, a one-room, four-grade institution with one middle-aged, conscientious teacher. In my class of eight kids, Charles Elkins was the best student. I was second best, always trying hard to be better than he was, but never quite managing. He could learn the month's poem faster than I could, do the arithmetic on the board more accurately, and beat me in spelling bees regularly. And after he did all that, he would give me the candy bar he got as the best speller and walk me home past the barn dogs that terrified me.

Charles (never Charley) was orphaned and lived with his sister, Mildred, with aging aunts and an uncle on a subsistence farm, about a mile up the road near the school.

At that time, farming, subsistence farming, was labor-intensive. Animals had to be fed and tended to—cows, chickens, pigs, horses, dogs. They had to be given water brought in buckets from the hand pump outside the house. Food was cooked from scratch, and cast-iron kitchen stoves were fed with wood, chopped and carried inside. Large gardens were essential for survival and needed planting and weeding. Crops had to be harvested, hay had to be cut, put into wagons, and brought to the barn for the livestock. Fences had to be mended; irrigation ditches that ran through the fields had to be dug open, kept free from silting up.

The grown-ups in Charles' family were good people, needing every bit of help they could muster. Charles and Mildred, from the time they were tykes, were essential to the survival of the farmers.

The farmstead, as I remember it, sat at the end of a long dirt lane, on the hillside, with some ramshackle outbuildings around the house and a huge barn. There was no yard, and the barnyard was full of muck and straw and animals. In the 1940s, the house had no indoor plumbing; all the water was carried inside and heated on the cookstove. There was little in the way of electricity. The toilet was outside and moved every couple of years when the holes filled up.

Charles and Mildred were fed and clothed and sheltered. But they worked hard. Before he caught the bus to school, where he was really good at chasing us during hide and seek, Charles had to muck out the horseshit in the barn and feed the pigs. His sister, Mildred, too, had chores, making the oatmeal and gathering the eggs. They both threw hay down to the cows and horses in the evening.

When the kids came to school, they smelled of sweat and manure, of rotting pig food and hay-muck. There was no running water inside the house, so the two of them had Saturday night baths so they would be "decent" for church, Pine Church, the next day. The rest of the week they wore the same clothes every day and washed hands and faces at night, in cold water, before bed.

At my house we had hot and cold running water and an upstairs bathroom with a tub. My father had a steady job in town, and my mother was a regular, "magazine-type" housewife: she washed and starched and ironed all our clothes, kept us clean and tidy, and sent us to school looking respectable. She had been a farm kid and knew that looking respectable kept kids out of trouble with the authorities. Her parents had lived a hand-to-mouth life on various rented farms mostly with no electricity or running water. At times, they had boarded rural school teachers, and Mom was scathing about the teachers' inability to deal with pumping water to take their baths and doing their business in spidery outhouses. She didn't allow teachers to be scornful of her children. We were always clean and starched and ironed, with a variety of clothes that we would wear to school.

Mrs. Gardner, the sole teacher of four classes in that one-room school, knew each of us as neighbors. She taught penmanship, showing us big swooping arm movements, and she played the piano and had us sing songs and recite poetry. Each class, 6 to 10 students, took turns at the recitation bench in front of the room, where they read aloud, practiced the alphabet on the blackboard, and were shown how to do arithmetic. While that was happening, the other 25 or 30 students filled out mimeographed sheets of addition and multiplication problems, passed notes back and forth, and (in my case) sneaked popcorn from my lunch bag and shared it with my seatmate. Mrs. Gardner came to the building at 5:30 AM to start the fire in the big potbellied stove. She rotated the chore of banging the blackboard erasers among the second and third graders, and sent the fourth graders in pairs down a weedy lane to a spring to bring drinking water back for the school. She went home after sweeping out the room, banking the fire for the night, and emptying the wastebaskets. By that time, the school bus had long left, making its last round, taking the Pine kids down the road.

But in fifth grade, we were bussed to Robb School, a big brick building near the factory where my father worked. It was in town, in a residential-industrial neighborhood, with cars and sidewalks and crosswalks at intersections. The school had a principal and hallways and separate rooms and teachers for each grade.

For me, town school was an astonishment; there was only one class per each big room; the whole day was given to just our class alone. At Goat Hill, I knew most of the lessons from fourth grade by the time I entered second. In town school, I didn't know what would come next. I was astounded by all the new ideas, new books, new arithmetic lessons. We were busy all day, doing schoolwork, reading aloud, answering questions from our history books, taking tests. It was never boring, and there were no long periods with nothing to do. We had our own moveable desks. Shelves in the room had brand new chapter books we could borrow. We were given our own textbooks for the entire school year; we didn't have to share them. We had new crayons and colored pencils. We had new songs to learn. There were new rules and real playground equipment. The toilets were inside and flushed.

The teacher liked me because I was clean and ironed and minded my manners.

But Charles smelt of manure and sweat. He wore the same clothes every day, and the clothes were patched and thin. The teacher made fun of him, washed his face in front of the class with a dirty rag. She mocked him as he started to stutter because of her bullying. She turned a bright, eager fifth grader into a sullen, angry kid.

I lost Charles that year, although I didn't consciously think about it. I reveled in the new, ever-interesting conditions of school, new kids, new ideas, new things to think about. I don't remember Charles walking me home past the Roadman dogs after town school. I sat by myself on the hour-long bus ride, observing people's houses, looking for flowers in the scrub along the road. I decided I was too big to be afraid of the barn hounds.

These days, teachers are taught to help bright children who come from homes that don't conform to middle-class standards. Breakfasts and hot lunches are available for them; school social workers help out with clothes and supplies. These days, Charles might have had a chance to leave the township, to get a good paying job, to excel and use his intelligence. But Charles, the smartest kid in our one-room school, became the county trash hauler, a garbage man. He could have been more than that.

The society also failed the Roadman girl, pregnant by her father at 13. And Bobby Burnham, whose intellectual challenges made him depend on his mother with no aid from outside the family. Pine Station and a variety of public schools showed me a cruel society in which I, in an accident of fate, thrived.

I love you.
Mama

November 18, 2020
Amorphinity

Dear Jan,

It's a gray day, full of leaves disintegrating in the rain, going from brown gold to muddy mush. An anonymous symphony on the radio booms and whines. In a fit of irritability this morning, I mopped the kitchen floor.

While mopping, I thought of the ways to clean floors—floors can be "washed," as Susan Saling would say, like bathing a baby or cleaning fine china. Sometimes they are "scrubbed," as in taking a toothbrush to the grout, crawling through suds on hands and knees.

But today I "mopped" the floor, using the stringy wet mop. Mopping is more serious than "flinging a mop at the dirt" but less fierce than scrubbing. I never, ever "wash" a floor because, in my lexicon, tracked-in muck and debris needs something more than washing.

While I mopped, I pondered other descriptions of days and ways. In Underwood-lingo, we talk about "shin-cracking days." On shin-cracking days, the universe puts sharp corners in our paths. "Shin-cracking days" led me to maunder on in my head about amorphous days, days which mush into fogs of disinclinations and dissatisfactions until, ouch, one catches one's shin on the edge of the coffee table. No one's fault, just that kind of day. Or days. Or weeks, months, the rest of one's life. Dear, dear. I *was* grumpy.

Luckily, my mind meandered further, from shin-crackers to thinking of other people who have lived seemingly amorphous lives. People have always had to deal with lives that seem to go on endlessly without much change. But traditionally, they take that mush and make shapes out of pilgrimages, marriages, and coming-of-age ceremonies and funerals. Farmers have marked the planting and harvesting seasons by the moon's presence, and great civilizations built astronomical wonders, buildings that captured an 18.6-year cycle (I'm thinking of the Puebloan peoples of the American southwest). The Puebloans marked their environment so that one specific day every 18.6 years, the sun rose between two large boulders. Its light traveled miles across the landscape to shine on a monumental building where, as it beamed through a window, it illuminated a special place on a far, dark wall. To everything, turn, turn, turn, there is a season. And the season, a mark in the mist, shapes otherwise shapeless time.

In my adulthood, I thought life would be a series of linear processes, culminating in achievements—getting a degree, owning a house, having a child, finishing an essay or a painting or a studio renovation. But as I aged, the line became less linear. Memories began to tangle with dailiness; the peonies lining the driveway in Kansas drift to memories of the violets lining the sidewalk in Wyoming and the iris along the back walkway in Pennsylvania. Here in Portland, the sedum lines the path to our front door.

Memories can work like cycles, marking similarities and differences and adding shape to our lives.

Mom always wanted flower gardens and worked fiercely around clay and children, hanging laundry, and making pot roast, to construct her paths of flowers. My gardening also requires tenaciousness, a refusal to give in to clay and aphids. I water when I don't want to and refuse to let arthritis and vertigo stop me from the joys of the work.

This continuity with my mother makes me see other things: "flinging a mop" is tied to a jolly insolence about housekeeping when other things, such as planting bulbs, are more important.

And so, circling back to this day, I have mopped the floor. I have watched my last blooming begonias mark time and seasons. When I go into the house, it will smell of Spic and Span, and the persimmon tree will glow outside the library windows. When you're finished, the floor is clean. The smell is good. And the golden autumn light shines on the mopped space.

Do smells and light make shapes? Did Mom look and revel in these same sensations? Is she watching me with smiling bemusement? Is the circle adequate to making the story?

Mama

December 26, 2020
Christmas Aftertastes

Dear Jan,

It's Saturday morning, Christmas was yesterday, full of texting and phone calls and a festive eggnog from the Salings. Today I move slowly. I am disconnected and dopey. We have a fridge full of chocolate truffles, brisket slices, scones and whipping cream, more than an aging body can digest. It's a slow and ponderous day, for which I am grateful.

Christmas is a tangled season for me. I remember the ecstatic thrills from my childhood and still feel pressure to reenact them in my middling-elderhood.

Christmas in Pine Station, when I was six and eight and ten, was magical, wild, delicious. Rituals—making lists, dreaming of presents, putting the bulbs on the Tree, the breathless line-up at the top of the stairs on Christmas morning, waiting to see the fully decorated rooms—were reenacted; the days were full of people and music. The tree lit the walls with color, the cooking turkey filled the house with exciting smells, the presents were glimpses of hope and the future— books, clothes, puzzles.

And then the Christmases we had with you, in Kansas, were good, although, because I did a lot of the planning, shopping, and decorating, they felt hard. I was working full time, overbooked, and harassed. The presents were never quite enough, even though they formed obscene piles around the tree. I had only myself to consult, and myself was always inadequate to the required magic.

These days, the family doesn't usually exchange gifts at Christmas. But this year, inspired, we wrapped two gifts for you. One was the result of seeing your photo of baking a pie in your cast-iron frying pan. We gifted you one of our old glass pie pans, writing that you could use it to cook and, also, to put under potted plants. And I found two delicately paint-ed bread plates, designed by your beloved friend, Mary Lou Goertzen, on eBay. I snatched them up, knowing that this was a real gift, something you would treasure.

You understood the humor of the pie plate, and you texted me to say you laughed when you unwrapped it. You were, you said, going to make a pie for dinner.

But you made no mention of the Mary Lou plates. I was puzzled, so this morning I texted you about them. You replied that you thought I was re-gifting *you* plates that you originally gave *us*—a *faux pas* in gift giving, at least to our family conventions. You were mistaken—you had given us a Mary Lou watercolor, not two of her plates.

You accepted my story about finding the plates on eBay, but I'm not sure you believed it. You apologized for not saying thank you; I accepted, but still I imagined you saying to Rick: "Mom must be losing it, she forgot that we were the ones who gave her these." I resigned myself to another less-than-sterling, gift-giving moment. And wondering if I was starting down the long road to dementia. So much for inspired gifting.

And so, my groggy feelings of the day after Christmas are accompanied by a wry sense of, once again, not managing the holiday well.

Today I should probably allow my yesterday's eggnog to percolate through my system, take *two* naps, and finish one of the four books sitting on the coffee table. Perhaps I've dealt with all the Christmas gifting nonsense I need to. I'm too old to take on so.

Mama

It's strange that Christmas can still evoke in me an anxiety that makes my heart pound. It has been years since I was responsible for Christmas magic. The family no longer exchanges gifts unless something is irresistible. My performance anxiety mimics that of my mother, who was in charge of Christmas back in Pine. She was given a set amount of money by my father, and of course the amount was too little, spread over too many who wanted too much. She had to have a festive dinner—and she hated to cook. She had to be fair to each child, while knowing that each of us had our own special needs. She worried and made lists and fussed and shopped and looked at our wish-lists. She bought candies and oranges and canned oyster stew for Christmas Eve (she hated oysters). She helped with church decorations, got us to choir practice, and made sure our choir gowns were cleaned and ironed for Christmas concerts.

I never had the burdens of five kids and a rambunctious household of hungry people, but I did have two birthdays on the 31st, Christmas, Kwanzaa, an occasional Jewish holiday when Jan was thinking of converting, and all this began with the horrors of Thanksgiving turkey. All in all, January's blank days were an enormous relief.

And in the middle of all this, a wise friend, older than myself, told me that I was the only one who cared; that no one was watching or waiting or anticipating that I would exceed myself this year, that I should stop wishing the tree to be more shapely, the lights more thrilling, the presents

207

more beautifully wrapped, or the turkey moist and flavorful. Only I was watching, and perhaps now, at my age, I could simply look away.

February 18, 2021
Stories and Identity

Dear Jan,

In Joan Didion's, *White Album*, she says *"We live, … especially if we are writers, by the imposition of a narrative line upon disparate images, by the 'ideas' with which we have learned to freeze the shifting phantasmagoria which is our actual experience."*

Stories, for me, are essential to clarifying that "shifting phantasmagoria," the mist of ongoing life in which I live. I understand why we elders tell stories—we have come to understand that things that simply were "what it was" at the time they happened, ultimately form a story—give some structure—to our lives.

We collect comparisons and use them to understand who we've become.

I was a country hick, a naïve hillbilly, who became a college professor, living in a city, enjoying string quartets and theater by Tom Stoppard. I never went to a museum or a professional concert or saw a real play until college. I never heard an opera that made any sense to me until age 32 when I moved to Kansas. Somewhere along the way, I slid away from my country origins and became the middle-class professional that shows up on my resume. And yet, I see clearly how much I retain of my country self.

Being from the hills of northern Appalachia meant not knowing how the middle class and the professional world worked. No one knew about colleges, why one would go there, what happened when you lived in dorms or confronted learned professors, or why professional honors societies were useful. No one had a sense of middle-class style, whether dress, architecture, or decor. No one but my mother read any books besides westerns, and no one, absolutely no one, ever used a cookbook. The furthest I traveled before 1966 was from central Pennsylvania to Ohio, where Uncle Al and his family lived. That uncle was the one who insisted that my family give me the $20 for Phi Beta Kappa membership; he had been to college and understood some of the rituals.

But the culture of my youth was clearly a culture. It had strong social and ethical rules. I learned most of those rules implicitly. I imbibed them while eavesdropping on women's kitchen talk or sitting around the table after dinner. Many of the ethical rules are still part of my conscience. However, I still have trouble slipping between the two worlds, places where neither the old nor the new are part of my bones.

These spaces make for humorous stories, but they are also evidence that I have lived between at least two worlds. I learned of differing societies on the fly, grabbing pieces of them as they went by.

Funerals are places where my different cultures were most obvious. My parents died in my late 40s and early 50s, in the 1980s and '90s. Jer and I were living in Portland at the time and the trips to our origins in northcentral Pennsylvania became the base for oft-told stories. Nowadays, funerals are generally private, with larger gatherings at memorials, where food and drink and stories are offered and photos and videos bring back memories. But, before memorials were common, especially in the hills of Pennsylvania, stern rituals governed death.

My father's funeral came first. It took place at Toby's, the local funeral home in the tiny town where he grew up. A viewing, a prescribed hour when people came alone or in small groups to view the dead person in the satin-lined casket, was held before the Christian service and burial procession. Family was expected to be present. What I did not know was that a family representative, generally one who was easiest with people, had to stand beside the casket with its laid-out dead to accept condolences of friends and acquaintances. As I lingered with my siblings at the back of the funeral parlor, my cousin Doris hissed: "June, get up front. People are waiting. You're the oldest!"

Startled, I looked around, saw that strangers were standing about, looking lost, and I obeyed Doris's order, scuttling to the front of the room. A silent line formed, each person stopping first to observe my dad's painted, still face, and then, patting me on the hand, they whispered their condolences. I thanked people whose names and faces I didn't know, and I fulfilled a duty I never knew I had.

Another unwritten rule, also about funerals, was that the family shouldn't "show off." No family member ever spoke publicly during the Christian service; doing so was a kind of self-aggrandizing, an interruption to the orderly transition of the soul into heaven. Nowadays, with memorial services celebrating the dead months after cremations, this rule feels strange. Back then, families sat silent in the front rows, expected to be overburdened with grief. At my mother's funeral, I violated that rule.

This violation and a humorous incident beforehand have become stories.

Some years after my father died, my mother followed him. Jer and I, coming from the West Coast for the funeral, had stayed with his sister, 10 miles from Toby's Funeral Home. The morning of the service, we left Beth's house early, hoping for coffee before the viewing. We had trouble finding anything open, but finally, along an old back road, we came across a store we had known many years before as a creamery, where ice cream was the attraction. That morning we saw it provided Eats—and coffee. We parked, relieved and cheerful that something out of our past was still alive. We went in. Our appearance in formal funeral attire stopped the assembled locals in mid-speech. We sat down at the counter; a harried waitress called me "dearie" and slapped coffee cups in front of us.

When we finished our coffee, we tried to catch her eye. We were running late. The only staff member in sight, she ignored us. Deciding to leave the money on the counter, I asked a guy in a red plaid shirt how much a cup of coffee cost.

He answered, in an exaggerated country drawl, "Generally speaking, one cup is $2.50."

I stared at him, disbelieving. (Remember, this was the 1990s.)

"That's for out-of-towners," he added. "Locals, we pay 75 cents."

Ah, gotcha.

I grinned, said we were on our way to my mother's funeral, and that made us locals.

We plunked down a couple of dollars, waved to the waitress across the room, and made our escape. Jer and I figured, as we got into the car, that we had satisfied a lot of coffee drinkers that morning; they would check the local paper to see who was being buried, check out the survivors' names, and we would be identified.

My mother's long slow decline into *Alzheimer's* meant we had already suffered the sharpest grief. That morning when we got to Toby's, I decided it was time to celebrate her release and mark the occasion with something of her old self.

Despite the disapproving head shakes of others, I decided to violate the seen-but-not-heard rule. I told the presiding pastor that I needed time on his program. I wanted to read a poem. I knew which one—Tennyson's "Crossing the Bar"— because my mother loved Tennyson and read his poetry to me when I was five and learning to iron. However, finding a copy of the poem in that town of 2,000 or so was a problem. There was no poetry in the books of Toby's parlor nor in the little drugstore that carried Hallmark Cards.

Family being family, they knew that the reading of this poem was important to me. I was "from away," and there was no telling what I might do if denied the chance. And they also knew that our mom would have liked a farewell poem.

Denise, my sister Carol's daughter, ran to her old high school up the street and caught her former English teacher between classes. He photocopied the poem for her, and she brought it back to Toby's, where the siblings, other relatives, friends, and curious strangers waited for the service to begin.

Because of my family, I could override the frowns, and standing in front of the assembled crowd, I read,

> "Sunset and evening star,
>   And one clear call for me!
> And may there be no moaning of the bar,
>   When I put out to sea,

But such a tide as moving seems asleep,
　　Too full for sound and foam,
When that which drew from out the boundless deep
　　Turns again home.

Twilight and evening bell,
　　And after that the dark!
And may there be no sadness of farewell,
　　When I embark;

For tho' from out our bourne of Time and Place
　　The flood may bear me far,
I hope to see my Pilot face to face
　　When I have crost the bar.

Although I didn't know it at the time, as my mother lay dying, Cousin Doris had read poetry to her, sitting at her bedside during those long hours. So I am comforted, thinking that my rebellion was accepted as a daughter's grief, appropriate if a bit untoward.

What to make of these stories? They capture, in funny little tales, something of that place and those people: unwritten but strict etiquette about funerals; local jokesters putting on outsiders; the surround of family, who will tell you what to do but also help you break the rules.

In addition, the stories explain something to me about human interactions in my current, professional, city culture.

I am still learning how to navigate a middle-class world of retired couples who give dinner parties. In Pine Station, people stayed for dinner or dropped in just before dinner time and expected to be fed. There were no "dinner parties."

I am an awkward participant in the memorial services for friends and parents of friends, not knowing quite what my role should be when there is no receiving line or whispered condolences. When there's an illness or death in the family, I don't know if I am expected to show up with food or comfort, or simply email my thoughts and not bother people who are already overburdened.

I am acutely aware of the stories that tell me, if only by contrast, who I might have been, and who I became instead. I continue to watch what others do, learning the etiquette of the moment and the people and the place. I am still tempted to do the unexpected, to read poetry at funerals, although now the gatherings are memorials, and such an action would just be boring. And so it goes.

Mama

VI

NOT DEAD YET

An aged man is but a paltry thing, / A tattered coat upon a stick, unless / Soul clap its hands and sing. —W. B. Yeats

June 16, 2019
The Fear of –

Dear Jan,

I seem to be working on these little notes as if they were real writings.

Oops, there's an ouch-phrase: "as if they were real writing." Popped up without a thought.

So, I chide myself. The writings are for sure "real," in the sense that they are words on the page, words which can be collected, collated, and read by another person. But "real" as in important, definitive, useful, funny, witty—oh dear, a whole 'nother tale. Which I can't quite talk myself into.

But then, another thought pops up: Ram Dass in his book, *Still Here*, says that we have to learn "to separate the fear of pain from the actual sensation." The fear that what I'm producing is not real is an anticipation of failure. My fear of failure can be separated from the actual work, which is the writing that I do as I sit here at my studio computer.

The fear that my writing is not "real" is a bit like the fear that when I'm a frail elder, I will be reduced to a stinking heap of flesh, lying in unwashed sheets. If anything is real, it's the fear embodied in the thought, not the actual stinking flesh. Nor does my fear that my words and sentences don't measure up to important literary production have any tangible being. The reality is in the tapping of my thoughts onto the keyboard and their mysterious appearance in front of me on the screen.

It's useful to separate both the fear of aging and the terror of not producing real writing from what is actual at this moment. Real writing in this immediate context is writing about what is happening right now. What *is* real at this moment is me, fleshy, upright, warm in my turtleneck and blue jeans and wrapped around by my shabby desk chair.

It is good to sit here typing with my studio door open so I can watch the rain on the hosta lilies outside the door. I write as I sense the lingering taste of raspberries (breakfast), weak tea (ah, liquid, tepid, moist), chattering rain, a fly against the windows, and the sound of typing clatter.

All these immediate sensations and surrounds are real. I am not a fake. The taste of coffee was real as are the hostas and the rain and the words accumulating on the computer screen.

Love,
Mama

June 26, 2019
"Still" as a Useful Term

Dear Jan,

About four years ago, I decided I needed to know what other people have written about aging.

One of the first books I read was by William Thomas, Dr. Bill as he calls himself. The book is *Second Wind: Navigating the Passage to a Slower, Deeper, and More Connected Life.*

Dr. Bill rants, as writers on elderhood are wont to do, about the stereotyping that happens when people talk about us elders. One of his beefs is the word "still." He tells us to stop the "stills" when talking or thinking about getting old.

No more "Still driving at 101? Still doing *The Times* Crossword Puzzle at 75? Still playing softball at 87? Still doing brain surgery? Still writing on Facebook?" Dr. Bill dislikes the incredulity of the direct questions: "Are you still running marathons?" "Are you still sleeping around?" (OK, I made that up, since I suspect no one over 60 is thought of as "still sleeping around" except by those over 75, who don't ask.)

Dr. Bill explains that this particular use of "still" reinforces the notion that normal behavior for everyone over the age of 40 is to be a "normal adult," to strive for middle-aged goals even as we are way beyond them. We should stop applauding the elders (who in fact may be ourselves) who manage to mimic (however badly) middle-aged behavior.

The word "still," used in this apparently admiring way, denies the reality of getting old. It hides the reality of our new life, one that is different from middle-age but which lasts just as long. Denying this new stage prevents us from understanding ourselves and from embracing our new states of being. When we elders imagine ourselves 59 instead of 77, according to Dr. Bill, it is pernicious. It refuses to give us a grip on our reality, and without that grip, we are reduced to mere shadows of something else. We do not still go about the world as if we were 60, and for this we should be grateful. Now it's time to sort out how we can live fully at age 80.

I liked Dr. Bill's rant against the use of "still" when I read it a few years ago; he definitely has a point about elderhood being a different stage of human development. Dr. Bill says we've got to abandon our desires to climb Mt. Rainier and to tour four cities in three days; we need to slow down, think deep thoughts, and be part of community; his mantra is "slow, deep, and connected."

But of course, still being the family argufier, I have to counter Dr. Bill's dislike of "still." I agree that I am no longer 60, but even as I have changed ages, I have some "stills" in me.

I still do art, albeit at a slower pace. I am still greedy for more plants, more friends, more interaction. My greed is often misbegotten, and my definition of "adventure" has changed. But I still like people, reading, talking, and thinking.

I have always been gregarious, finding it amazing that people with ideas and traditions new to me are out there and can be brought into my life. As a landscape observer and painter, deserts stun me, just as the rolling blue Appalachians do, although I no longer hike the trails. I can still visit the edges of others' existences and check out websites with photos. I can't meet people in conferences and bars, but I can meet my neighbors. I don't fly across countries anymore, but now know that the aging of the "little boxes" architecture in my own neighborhood is as good as knowing about the castles in Wales. In other words, I have had to change how I encounter and think about people and ideas and adventures, but the desire to encounter and think is *still* strong in me.

I don't want to be what I was as a striving working adult. I resist being the amazing example of an 80-year-old who doesn't look a day over 70. I will never be the outlier woman who runs marathons at 90 (I did mine at 50), nor Matisse, scissoring masterpieces on his deathbed.

But I like looking out from my old eyes, investigating the world from my new stage of development. I can think cheerfully about Slow, Deep, and Connected, but I also *still* have old notions of self.

I've decided that "still," used properly, is useful. We alter subtly, not wholly, at different stages of development, whether we are going from being 5 to 20 or 30 to 69. Some parts get thrown away, some are enhanced, some fall off, some simply wither away. Maybe we will abandon Saturday night drinks and bar hopping but will retain our love of watching the crazy antics of the youngers on TV. Maybe we will continue to study our relationships, even while they don't involve sex and intense discussions of the future.

This morning, Jer and I went to Freddy's discount store and bought a trunkload of plants. It is, after all, only June, so planting more is a no-brainer. I'm still greedy for boxes of bedding plants to fill in the holes in my already loaded gardens. Still greedy to argue with experts about their expertise.

And Jer reminds me that Dr. Bill is a lot more sophisticated and subtle in his work than I grant him, and that setting him up as a foil is fine, but I shouldn't get too greedy about having a fake target to put down. And so, my thinking still has to be worked on a bit.

With grins,
Yer Ma,

I am the family "argufier," one who takes exception to whatever is being said just because another idea about the topic popped into my head. Spouse Jer, grandson Sam, and daughter Jan all recognize this tendency and either look at me resignedly, or (and I find this more fun) argue back, pointing out the flaws in my hastily, sometimes poorly thought, notions. I have done this all my life, and it certainly shows in the way I understand and approve of Dr. Bill's "still" while arguing that I am still greedy for more life.

July 1, 2019

Slow, Deep, and Engaged: The Popcorn Mind

Dear Jan,

Now I have to ruminate further about Dr. Bill's "slow" (remember the mantra "slow, deep, and connected"?). It's an easily remembered set of words and sometimes feels right.

But maybe "slow" needs further examination.

Physically speaking, we are definitely slowing down, something I mostly don't celebrate. But there are other kinds of "slow:" Dr. Bill talks of slow money, slow medicine, slow food, slow cities, and slow sex. I like his ideas about those topics. What he doesn't speak to, though, is thinking, ideas, the mind that takes in the world and analyzes and reanalyzes it.

For me, this is the popcorn mind, where thoughts bounce around, sometimes coming across teeth-challenging kernels, but sometimes, also finding a bowl of chewable goodies.

Last night, at another of the Northwest Chamber Music Festival concerts, instead of concentrating on the music, I was mulling over James Woods' essay about a recent translation of *War and Peace*. Our reading group is currently dealing with *War and Peace,* and, in preparation for the discussion, I found the Woods essay. So, popcorn-like, my mind bounced back and forth between the concert sounds and the ideas in Woods' analysis of the novel.

The concert featured a splendid clarinet soloist who hit notes I thought came from the bassoon. He did jazz riffs. One of his cadenzas had me in tears. I momentarily forgot about *War and Peace* and reveled in sound.

However, the second half of the program featured Mozart's *Clarinet Concerto in A Major*—33 long minutes. I've heard a lot of Mozart, in concert and on classical radio stations, through my collection of CDs, and whenever a music programmer is in need of a quick fix. Last night I was bored by Mozart.

The *Clarinet Concerto in A Major* repeats itself. It has repetitions. A lot of repetitions. The orchestra plays variations on a theme, seemingly *ad infinitum*, and then the clarinet joins in, sometimes carrying the theme loudly, sometimes blending in with the other musicians, but generally speaking, just forming another repeat of the motif. Finally, another theme will start up, and the repetitions will begin and go on until, under some circumstances, sleep rather than music fills my head.

So after the concert, lying in bed, I was wide awake, writing indignant editorials on the hell of musical repetition and boring concerts—and then a thought popped up.

I remembered a story you told about a songfest you were part of, a Jewish one, if I'm remembering correctly. The rabbi got everyone singing a phrase, over and over, using his conductor's authority to direct the sing-along, making the group repeat the notes in different keys, start on different notes, softer, louder, more somber, more joyous, on and on, until the variety of singers became a single body, totally focused on him to achieve oneness. And then, just as it appeared that the height had been reached and nothing more could be done, the rabbi stopped and allowed a long silence to linger.

Then he looked at the group and said: "That's great! That was wonderful! Now," another long pause—"it's time to start singing."

On he went with that same tune, carrying the stunned singers with him for another 15 minutes. By then, the glory was greater, the subtleties more understood, the variations finer, and the group was even more finely honed.

And I remembered those Mozart repetitions, the variations, the subtle and not-so-subtle ways that he keeps us attentive, provided that we allow ourselves to fall into the repetitions. The key is to forget the rest of the world, to fall into the sounds, to allow the repetitions to embed and change and become new because of their minute alteration.

With my midnight popcorn brain, I remembered Woods' analysis of *War and Peace*—he says that we believe in the cast of characters in Tolstoy's novel; we laugh and cry with them and want to join the family. We immerse ourselves in their stories. And yet, Woods writes, the characters are mere repeats of types—the young romantic female falls in love with the wrong man; a foolish young man goes merrily off to war where other young men try to kill him. That young, sweet female turns into a matronly mother; the brash young fellow survives the war and becomes a middle-aged estate manager. The types are mere repetitions of human beings as we know them. But we are enthralled with Tolstoy's variations, we exalt with his characters and mourn with them and gasp in horror when they are faced with trauma. We become immersed in the repetitions of types because we are caught up in the variety, the subtleties, the fine honing.

It's Tolstoy who carries us along. It's Mozart who pulls us into his repetitions. It's the rabbi who pulls the singing group into an impossible number of ways to move through the phrases. Enthrallment is a matter of immersing ourselves and forgetting that we repeat. Humans repeat but with infinite variation, immense subtleties, ongoing pleasures, singular in the variety.

All that popped around and around in my head, along with the Mozart and my memories of you and I talking about music, and *War and Peace*, and then I put Dr. Bill in. I had slowed physically (with bits of music repeating in my memory), but my brain still popped like popcorn.

"Slow" isn't always the correct mantra, at least with Mozart and Tolstoy and enraptured choirs jumping around in one's aged brain. Dr. Bill needs an addendum. "Slow with variations," perhaps.

Mama

I don't know if everyone lingers over their thoughts, thinking them over and over, refining and arguing with them, pulling the events of the day into the night, thinking about why Mozart, so beloved, felt boring, and why War and Peace *is such a classic when it uses boilerplate stories. Mozart's clarinet concerto and Tolstoy's novel get fitted into a story about group singing, and they all relate to each other and my life; my interior world connects itself to bigger, more interesting worlds. I expand.*

August 5, 2019
And What About Art?

Dear Jan,

You may have noticed that, despite my being a working visual artist, most of these posts are not about art but about the quotidian, the way we live our lives, about flowers and trees and plants. The gardens, it turns out, are an extension of my studio artwork. They involve decisions about form, shape, color, line, rhythm, texture, intentionality—and creativity.

The more I garden, however, the less control I have over how things will turn out. I do not understand why only zinnias and allium stay alive under the persimmon tree. Nor can I figure out why, in the big front bed, some soil is soft and friable, while next to it is unbudgeable clay. Plants that bloom wildly and gloriously one summer sink into sulks the next. A plant I stuck into the ground a few years back suddenly bursts forth, putting all around it to shame, but upending my carefully designed color scheme.

One moment, earlier this year, I came out the back door of the garage into the side walkway, a path lined with a rotting fence on one side, and the air conditioner and recycling bins on the other. At that moment in late June, in opening the door, I was dazzled by beauty. Overnight the red-pink valerian had climbed the fence; at the end of the walkway, honeysuckle blooms and greens leaves smothered the rough bark of the dogwood tree, from whose largest branch a pot overflowed with purple petunias. The persimmon leaves glowed lime-green with sunlight, coreopsis and zinnias danced in yellows and oranges, and a couple of tall lilies poked their heads around the corner of the house. It was an astonishing sight; it filled my vision, right up to my brain's edges. I was gobsmacked.

And that's why I love gardening. One works and works, and tries and tries, and then, in the most unexpected moment and space, comes the reward—a vision beyond one's intentions, complete and whole.

Which brings me to more conventional visual art. I have spent the last five months working with ink and paper. I had no idea what I was doing when I began but was taken with the texture of paper and the ways ink was absorbed. I sprayed and poured and blew air over blue, black, and sepia ink blobs, layering, seeing how various papers spread and patterned the color. I sampled extensively. I liked what I was seeing.

Then—I got stuck. I was no longer interested in the patterns, but I couldn't think of what to do next. Stuck.

But, like the unexpected peeping out of the lily bloom, I found a different tool to pull the ink across the paper. Back I went—pouring, spraying, ordering new papers, trying new possibilities.

This morning, I came out and before I began this writing, I cropped a paper piece hanging on the design wall, estimated what I needed to do next, cut up some watercolor paper to make a new shape, and thought about what I could try.

Inside the studio, I garden my designs. In the garden, I design the blooms. I revel in the making and the unexpected that comes out of the process, failures and all. I like the splayed sepia ink as it runs into the green-black of dried lines, the green leaves and pink valerian against the rotting gray fence. Quotidian: immediate, passing joys.

Love you,
Mama

September 9, 2019
Maggie and Millie and Reading with Friends

Dear Jan,

"Maggie and Millie and Molly and May / Went down to the beach one day to play."

Today, our reading group is reading poetry—eight poems, one for each member of the group. We will spend a couple of hours playing with language, rhythm, rhyme, periods, and commas—all the fun stuff that short sentences, holding compressed ideas, can contain.

If you read and re-read a poem often enough, lines from it will stick in your head. Today, the worm-words in my head are "Maggie and Millie and Molly and May."

But of course, when the earworm plays, the words get changed, so is it "Went down to the beach one day to play" or "Went down to the beach to play one day?" Or "Went down to play at the beach one day?" Pop music puts earworms into me in the same muddled way as poetry of this sort does, although in music the melody is the thing, and the muddling of text not very important.

However, poets write poems exactly the way they want them to be read. The curse of the reader is to scratch her head through the rhythms and rhymes trying to remember which way, play or day, finishes the couplet. And then, perhaps and if it's a reading with a group, to think about why the poet did it as she did—why that choice and not this?

cummings-the-poet resolved the question of "play" / "day;" all we readers have to do is to think about it. The joy of being with this group of people is that we have the time, the space, and the desire to listen to each other and share personal knowledge and thoughts. We give and take freely and can bring our whole living experiences to the subject.

So "Maggie and Milly and Molly and May, / Went down to the beach one day to play."

Only—and exasperatingly to me at this moment—it's actually

"Maggie and Milly and Molly and May
Went down to the beach (to play one day)

Punctuation makes a written-out poem visual—missing periods, lowercase names, and added parentheses are this case in point. Punctuation is never boring with cummings. He forces us to see as well as recite. Who knew that Milly and Maggie could be so full of fun in their tiny trip to the beach? Only those who are observing closely the poem, their own rendition, and how it trippingly tripped up their tongues.

Cheers, (Mama)

September 26, 2019
The Coming Dark and Other Maunderings

Dear Jan,

As I sit here in the studio, I can swivel around on my chair and look at the art I've made. Paintings lean against the walls and furniture, the wire sculpture sways in the breeze of the fan, the silk crows on the quilted fabric still stare at the double moon, something they've been doing for 15 years or more.

My most recent ink-on-paper piece started with dark inked lines, made with pens, with brushes, and with sticks and fingers. The marks began as lines; they meandered, circled, straightened, and often tangled with other lines, but they were still black lines to be followed around the paper.

When these lines are applied with a lot of liquid, the primary marks branch into wicking tributaries. The more liquid the ink is when it gets pulled across the sheet, the more it wicks away from its primary black mark. But always, there remains a strong, dark inner line.

The second component of this ink piece is the opposite of line. It's a poured, smeared, misted mass of blacks and grays. It's watery ink, sponged over or brushed with a four-inch house brush, misted and sprayed over the dried lines. The mists and smears coat the lines but don't obliterate them. The two elements, the stark linear against the misted brushings, play off one another.

This art piece reminds me of something of my ongoing existence, the way I now live my life. Yesterday I had another bad vertigo attack, and the day was wiped over by dizziness. Parts of it I can remember, but during most of it I was too fuzzy to make much sense of anything. The day had no shape or structure. Then, today, that fog lifted, and my life went toodling along in its ordinary way, marked with food and companionship and music and writing—what we think of as the usual lines of life.

I imagine that that could be one way to think about death, the coming dark, when the dark lines of our little life are overtaken by larger mists and fogs.

Bill Stafford, in his poem "The Way It Is," uses a textile metaphor to describe the lines that compose our lives.

> There's a thread you follow. It goes among
> things that change. But it doesn't change.
> People wonder about what you are pursuing.
> You have to explain about the thread.
> But it is hard for others to see.
> While you hold it you can't get lost.
> Tragedies happen; people get hurt
> or die; and you suffer and get old.

Nothing you do can stop time's unfolding.
You don't ever let go of the thread.

Mama

Vertigo attacks have been with me since 1982 and were the cause of my retirement on disability in 1985; the worst vertigo symptoms were with me continuously during the late 1980s and early 1990s; they wiped out my short-term memory, my ability to talk easily and sometimes even to walk without aid. I no longer could comprehend much of what I read.

When I came to Portland in 1989 and was finally diagnosed, I had two of the bad vestibular canals plugged. This surgery allowed me to come back from a house-bound existence. I took up art, which kept me learning and occupied whenever I could do the physical work. The art brought me back to life, and because of it, I have managed to be as content as most other humans who have lived this long. The thread, thick and thin, continues.

January 7, 2020
I Want Something....

Dear Jan,

The root canal is mostly out of the way, and I am in the mood for retail therapy. Alas, I can't think of a thing I want to buy.

Remember how Sam used to say, "I want something." He could never tell me what he wanted, any more than I can figure out what I want. I just want something.

Inchoate yearnings—seems to be a universal state.

Perhaps it's a desire to move on, to be part of some energized group going fiercely toward a goal, rather than stuck in a boring quotidian. In my recent reading, I came across a phrase: something like "paintings observe; writing acts." But this writing doesn't seem to involve action.

The not-endingness of these notes, as compared to my finished visual art, is clear. The becoming-ness of writing makes me yearn for something, an endpoint. A retail therapy of sorts, where the package arrives and the underwear is pronounced perfect, stowed away in the cupboard, and for a minute or two, one (me, I mean) *has* something.

Susan B. Anthony shared a quip with Elizabeth Cady Stanton, saying that at age 80 they would be perfect; they both died at age 86, without reporting on their status vis-à-vis perfection. I notice that my writing is always up for more editing, never perfect, and so, like Stanton and Anthony, it is always becoming. Paintings watch me; writing is my continuing journey.

Hugs,
Mama

January 8, 2020
A Day In-Between

Dear Jan,

I found the quote I paraphrased last night. My memory was off. The original is much better:

Paintings think, language works.

Paintings and visual art face outward, observing the viewer in silence; writing seeds itself within its readers, chatting away, challenging and changing the reader's on-going mind.

Paintings are finished. Whole in themselves, they are stopped.

But language is linear. Words are read one after another. They set up vibrations and rhythms and then change them as they move to new sentences and paragraphs and pages. Language, moving through time, encourages the mind to do likewise.

Mama

The phrase I use above is from A Novel Bookstore, *by Laurence Cossé. The original quote is in a collection of aphorisms and essays by George Perros:* Papier Colle: Paper Collage. *Books within books, thoughts within thoughts, essays about thoughts coming from books about books.*

January 12, 2020
Old People's Projects, According to John McPhee

Dear Jan,

John McPhee, 10 years older than Jer and I, recently published a short piece in *The New Yorker* about why we elders keep on keeping on.

McPhee's *raison d'etre* for writing this particular essay is to ponder a student's question to another writer, Thornton Wilder. The elderly Wilder was asked about his current research and writing project: "Why would you want to do that at your age?"

McPhee thought the question deserved an answer (Wilder refused to deal with it). Definitely a young guy's question, says McPhee, and at the time, he had no answer. However, at age 88, he has figured it out.

The point of Wilder's project, was, according to McPhee "to extend Thornton Wilder's life.... It beat dying. It was a project meant not to end."

And then McPhee gives us examples of other projects meant not to end:

"George H. W. Bush jumped out of airplanes on his octo birthdays. Some people develop their own Presidential Libraries without experiencing an *a priori* need to be President. For off-spring and extended families, old people write books about their horses, their houses, their dogs, and their cats, published at the kitchen table. Old-people projects keep old people old. You're no longer old when you're dead."

And so, I write these bits of notes to you. So long as I am writing, I am not dead.

Always good to have someone validate one's own projects.

June

June 18, 2020
Doodling Toward Narrative

Dear Jan,

My writing these days resembles doodling more than painting. Instead of forming a grand canvas, covering a fantastic landscape, I use a sharpened pencil to make lines and shapes and then set the page aside, done without fanfare or meaning.

Doodling is random. Each morning I sit at the breakfast table and make lines that swoop or sweep or swerve. I like doodling because it has no intentionality. It starts randomly and generally finishes that way. All I need is paper and a sharpened pencil, and some engagement with the mark-making. Fun that does not require coherence.

But today I'm missing the pointedness of stories, of finely finished doodles, and the beginning-middle-end of essays. I miss the impact of the resonating chords of the landscape painting. I want to know where these writing doodles are going.

Mama

January 1, 2020
A Beamish Quotidian

Dear Jan,

Today is another day and in my quotidian, I am sitting, wholly caffeinated, listening to a bouncy Beethoven, *Piano Concerto #4*, on the radio. The bumptious piano is anchored by the concerto's orchestra. *Piano Concerto #4* makes me beamish.

"Beamish" is a word the family uses often. I don't need to remind you that it comes from Lewis Carroll's "Jabberwocky." Carroll took "beam," as in "light," and added "ish." "My beamish boy" is our hero (who took his vorpal sword in hand) as a ray of light: the narrator, his father, rejoices: "O frabjous day! Callooh! Callay!" chortling "in his joy." And thus, we have all the good words for rejoicing, with frabjous and callooh and callay and beamish, tootling alongside the Beethoven.

But ah, *Piano Concerto # 4* has concluded, and a somber violin is lamenting something, at a very slow pace.

I find the lamenting violin tiresome. I imagine my friends, historians, and students of music accusing me (although only in my imagination) of liking the banal and bouncy, only beamish Beethoven, never lamenting Schumann.

But of course, my guilt is self-induced, since the friend I imagine making such an accusation is the one who introduced "Jabberwocky" to our Proust-reading group. The group agreed it is a fine poem and "beamish" a worthy word, to be used in our quotidian lives.

So there, I've come to it, the point of today's quotidian. However familiar, the quotidian can be fun, even beamish— making decisions about which socks best mirror the weather, turning the day's schedule into a bit of nice phrasing: "writing, walking, listening, cooking," and then, writing to you while bouncing in my chair, part of the quotidian as a beamish activity.

Yer Ma,
June

Ah yes, I use "quotidian" a lot. It's a word I love, meaning "daily" or "routine." Some think it's a pejorative term: "He's a lazy slob who thinks of nothing but the next NFL game—nothing but the quotidian interests him." I think of it as good; focusing on the quotidian is an alternative to grasping for more, striving to become stronger, greater, to have a long article on your accomplishments in Wikipedia.

If you say the word aloud, you too may come to love quotidian. Quo-tid-ee-en. Trip it off your tongue lightly, and it will make your day.

Tuesday, October 20, 2020
Narrative

Dear Jan,

I continue to want to create "story," narrative, a beginning, middle, and end, character development and change. "We tell ourselves stories to live," to quote Joan Didion, again.

People love stories. My father and sister turned the events of their lives into tales, amusing family and friends. They regaled us with plot and self-deprecation that caused explosions of laughter. And through that, they consoled themselves.

Proust and Joyce, writers of autobiographical fiction, have slow plots, but we readers add up the storyline—Marcel (Proust) steps up on the curb and discovers his life's work (the book we have just finished); Joyce sends alter-ego Bloom home to make love to Molly, who says, "Why not?" "Yes."

Their stories don't wrap with the triumph of "Reader, I married him," but modernists as we are, we know how the writer's life unwinds. The ending of their stories is the book we hold in our hands.

In a panic, I ask myself—have I milked all the stories of my life, hence, no more narratives? Or is it the pandemic and the Trumpmare, the seeming endlessness, that wrings us out of tales. Am I too old for epiphany and change, or is it these contemporary conditions that interfere with the comforting fictions?

Do we tell stories in order to delude ourselves?

And then I remember the tulip bulbs, waiting to be planted so that we can look forward to their spring magic. And I think of the garden full of slugs, drowned in beery drunkenness, a battle never won but still worth pursuing. The drama of a spring full of color and triumph over ravaging beasts.

Guess I will have to make my own excitement. I will go catch slugs.

Hugs,
Mama.

December 10, 2020
The Canoe of June

Dear Jan,

Yesterday, I was scheduled to send images to my art buddy Jay; by noon today, I had emailed him details of the work in progress, received his faintly mysterious response, and continued with further work on the piece.

This work in progress is wire mesh, hand molded into a canoe shape. The shape sent me haring off into thoughts about the Ship of State (which listed badly but may slowly be hauled upright); the Ship of Fools (on which we are all gathered, sailing into the unknown); and the Canoe of June, with its leaky mythologies and history.

The wire canoe is a container, a vessel in the shape of a vessel. Perhaps there's a link to Freudian notions about my gendered love of containers; certainly there's personal history in my liking of that canoe shape. The piece will be about five feet long, three rectangular pieces of wire, folded and sewn together at their edges, then bent into the long oval shape.

I grew up in an age of clunky aluminum canoes (just past the era of wooden ones, but before kayaks were widely available). We spent a lot of summers playing in canoes. We launched them through slippery rocks and mud, jumped in, and rocked them wildly as we paddled to the middle of streams, pushed siblings over their sides, fell into rivers and lakes, and tried to climb back into them without tipping over. A famous family saga involves a canoe trip down the Owassee Rapids in the Pine Creek Gorge in frigid April. Jer and I were one pair of canoeists, and we ended up in the rushing, 45-degree water; I was newly pregnant with you but didn't know it. We didn't suffer from hypothermia, or at least it wasn't fatal, but it was certainly a fool's adventure. Good story, though.

Perhaps the tippy nature of canoes can be metaphorically carried to almost everyone's life—or as meditation guru Andy would say, thoughts and moods are constantly changing; our anguish this morning could be lost in a delight this evening. And vice versa. The canoe could ride the ripples or sink in a standing wave.

Many thinkers and writers have noted this. But not many have put together their own wire-mesh canoe, a leaky vessel indeed.

Verbalizing on an art project can easily doom its creation. But meh. I have been making containers—vessels—for a long time. In 2018 I worked extensively with wire; long before that I sewed fabric onto flexible wire mesh and shaped bowls and vases.

If you ask me why I am making this art, I have no answer. But, by the time I have the canoe filled with objects, I may have come up with a theme, an idea of what is intended. Or at least I will have something that I will invent words about, even if that is not what it means or where it came from.

The Canoe of June,
Hugs,
jou

January 4, 2021
January Light

Dear Jan,

All my life I have been obsessed with light—sunlight, moonlight, streetlight, incandescent bulbs and candles and fluorescent lights, hushed and quiet light, summer's noonday blaze and winter's cool dimness—I can *feel* light.

Living in Portland, Oregon, through the dim light of January makes me yearn for more.

Do you remember the prof whose art history class you and I audited, she who spoke of the gorgeous Portland light? The art teacher taught at PCC Sylvania, which is high on the edge of a hill, where the view opens up. The clouds are often contoured with gold. In that wide sky, the wind pushes the light around; even the lowering January light can flash and flare.

However, at this time of year, inner Portland near the river has a dim, dreary light. It is an evenly spaced gloom. It casts no shadows. In this tree-ridden valley, under the Doug firs and dank oaks, the light is an endless grey, a moist veil that mutes color and presses down. The wet air muffles browns and greens, making them indistinguishable.

I dwell on light on this January day, as I often do in January, because it's a piece with long drizzly days, where time, like shadows and highlights, are suspended. January has always seemed to be the longest month, going on and on; the fog hangs over the streetlights, the skies are never really dark, but are never really light. In January, light and time slow to drizzles and mist.

The outside Christmas lights, still hanging, allow us to pin down the lightness or dimness of the day. While they are programmed to turn off at dawn and light up at dusk, in January some lights don't see any dawn at all. A few turn themselves off at 10 AM—when the white house next door reflects and brightens the space. Others coil back into themselves at noon, invisible until evening brings them back to their cheerful glow.

For us, the lights mark the day's erratic march through time, a bit as the window notches on the homes at Chaco Canyon, in 900 AD, marked time. Those notches told the residents about the rotations of the sun through the equinox and solstice and how close or how far it was from the time when the daylight would lengthen, and the world would turn brighter with the sun's return. Our holiday lights are also useful.

Now it's time to drink tea and stop wallowing in gray sentiments. I am sitting in the studio, with my bright fluorescent lights shining all around me. The radio is playing Mozart. Outside, a little table glistens in the rain. The rain sparkles on its red slats; it reflects the mist and brightens it.

Thank heavens for red tables and multi-colored Christmas lights and Mozart as well as for the wet muted days of January.

"Death is the mother of beauty" says Wallace Stevens, and moist mist and drizzly rain is the mother of growth.

Hugs,
Mama

January 23, 2021
Delusions to Get By

Dear Jan,

I have grown fond of Marilyn's metaphor for sitting down and typing with no particular idea in mind: she calls it "clearing the throat."

So this morning, I am clearing my throat.

The Proust reading group has started James Joyce's *Ulysses*, which I have been dreading for years. I knew it would come to this: any group that starts with Proust's *In Search of Lost Time* was bound to take up Joyce, if not *Finnigan's Wake*, then at least *Ulysses*.

To my astonishment, I am loving it. Not the characters. Nor the plot (such as it is). Even the language does not really enthrall me. What I am loving is the thinkiness of *Ulysses*, parsing out meanings and allusions and word play within it. *Ulysses*, thus far, is a giant jigsaw puzzle with classical gleanings from Plato and Shakespeare and early church fathers; newly imagined ("agenbite of inwit") word play; images of an early 20th century port city with the river Liffey and the Irish sea; and even music—ballads, naughty bar songs, and opera—these can be checked out on the internet and listened to through scratchy old recordings. All of these bits (explained by scholars) are part of the story that Stephen Dedalus is living.

Dedalus is a tormented academic, too high-minded to pray when his dying mother asks him to but racked with guilt because he's so sensitive to his insensitivity. This leads him to all kind of parsings of Catholicism (which he has renounced) along with sardonic observations about Ireland and England, the nature of the snotgreen sea, and so forth. Each of Dedalus's maundering requires me to have three online sources, as well as a cheat-sheet. The internet's definitions and translation sites are extremely useful. A "costdrawer" is, wonderfully, an accountant; Arius is a heretic in Roman Catholic dogma, whose words were seen as poison. He met a scatological end on a public toilet seat, the kind of detail that makes me cackle.

None of what I've found matters, and that's perfect. Poor old Stephen Dedalus, tormented Irishman, who knows more than I've forgotten—an ineluctable modality of the grazing, unengaged reader. My bosom heaved not a single time. Not a single tear dripped from my sleepy eyelids.

And so, a shiny day with a big book, a cup of hot coffee, and a few nuts for cozy comfort.

Yer Mum

March 14, 2021
Reviewing

Dear Jan,

I have begun reviewing my 2019 writings, thinking about bringing these meanderings to a close. And I am bemused.

Bemused today by how in the beginning I had used those concepts, "slow, deep, connected" to frame my thinking about my life—and then, how I modified that to maundering about meditation and *"letting it go,"* to find a way out of the fear of the future, to exist within the present. Finally, I began chasing the notion of story, of narrative. I wanted, I want, to write about the present in such a way as to shape it, to find structures in the mist and sculpt them into forms that make sense.

We are almost at the end of our personal pandemic and isolation, although the re-entry will probably be slow and cautious. On March 17 I turn 79; I began these writings almost two years ago. Time, that old trickster, has done it again.

Mama

March 17, 2021
Today is the Last Day....

Dear Jan,

Today I am 79—I am entering my 80th year. Astounding. This happens only to other people.

But here I am.

Also, today I get my second Covid-19 shot and can feel freer and less anxious about the virus that has pinned us down for this last year.

And today I am closing out this set of letters to you.

It's been a crazy couple of years—reading and reviewing written materials on aging, His-and-Her cancers, the Covid-19 pandemic, the insurrection and storming of the Capitol on January 6, Donald Trump's attempted coup, Joe Biden's election and a return to hope for the democracy— and our continued march or slither or trundle or thunder into the next day.

The sun is shining, it's supposed to be in the 60s today, Kyla-the-gardener comes tomorrow. I will probably be in the throes of Covid-shot reaction. And our pandemic anxiety will be relieved. So it's a good ending to these letters to you, a long time coming.

I love you. But you know that. I've had an interesting time with this writing. You may have guessed that. Now I get to go back and edit and delete and ponder what I said and try to say it better. And then I will wrap the writing into a package and I will give it to you.

With all my love,
Mama

AUTHOR'S NOTE

"You get old and you realize there are no answers, just stories." Garrison Keillor

Youth wants to know what it all means.

Adults think they'll figure it out later on.

And elders (me, I mean) know that someone will make a good quip, and we'll be off the hook.

And so, praise the day, tell the stories, watch the crows, and catch up with your friends. Slow, deep, and connected. No answers; just stories.

It's all yours, all you have left, so give one of your habits a good story. And when that's told, move on to another. And don't forget the crows.

ACKNOWLEDGEMENTS

Many people heard me out about this project as it began, advanced, and took various shapes. Among the most dedicated were Marilyn Gottschall, who, in reading the work, provided me with much to think about, both in ideas and life. She also forced me to decide how often I dared to use the word "quotidian." Minna Doskow also kindly read and made encouraging comments on a large part of the manuscript.

I spend a lot of time talking about kinwork in the "reports" and I am grateful that I live in a neighborhood with good people who indulge me in my gregarious, sometimes irrepressible, neighboring. Among them are John and Susan Saling, Dan and Mary Graves, and Kerri and David Weatherby.

And while Jan Underwood was not afforded a single glimpse of the writing as it went along, her presence in my life is clear. She is also the most published author in the family, having written five novels, among them *Heartless* and *Fault Lines*, which can be found online as well as from your favorite bookstore. She is one of my heroes.

Finally, and most importantly, Jer Underwood spent innumerable hours listening to me read bits and pieces of the various entries. He read at least three drafts (of varying sizes) of the full manuscript. And as he read, he edited. And copyedited. And consulted. And never said a discouraging word. He's my guy.

ABOUT THE AUTHOR

June Underwood is a middle-old woman living in Portland
Oregon, in an old suburb where the houses are small, the
children cheerful, and the chickens loud. She has been a college professor, a visual artist, a kinworker, and a writer. Also,
she is the wife of Jer (for almost 60 years), grandmother of
Sam, and the mother of Jan, the Real Jan.

Made in the USA
Middletown, DE
25 April 2023

29264829R00146